SHAPED NOTES

Praises for Larnelle Harris

"We throw around words like 'integrity,' 'the real deal,' 'what you see is what you get,' and 'family values.' Use all of those, and throw in 'a world class talent' and you have Larnelle Harris. What an artist! What a genuine spirit! What a class act!"

— **Bill Gaither**, ASCAP Songwriter of the Century,
Gospel Music Hall of Fame Inductee

"Larnelle Harris has inspired people around the world with his unique singing gift. But wait until you read about the surprising journey that God took him on. Your own life will be touched by his story!"

— **Pastor Jim Cymbala**, Brooklyn Tabernacle, Brooklyn, New York

"I'm a fan of Larnelle's exquisite voice. He has been abundantly blessed by God with an enormous amount of talent. This book, he has written about his life, is captivating and remarkable, and I thank him for sharing his story."

— **Barbara Mandrell**, Country Music Hall of Fame Inductee,
3-time Entertainer of the Year

"When I think about the 32 years I have known Larnelle, there is a saying that comes to mind…'Let your choices reflect what you say your priorities are.' Larnelle is the epitome of this. As we have traveled together over the years, he would often choose to drive for hours rather than stay in a hotel, just so he could be home, even for a short time. The next day he'd get right back in the car and drive to wherever we were for a concert that evening. I count it one of the great joys in my life to not only sing with Larnelle over the years, but to call him my friend."

— **Sandi Patty**, Most Awarded Female Vocalist
in Gospel Music History

"It has been a joy, honor and privilege to know and be ministered to by my friend, Larnelle Harris. He has humbly lived a life of integrity and used his gifts to advance the glory and goodness and worship of God to the benefit of His people. He has truly lived a life worth living."

— **Dr. Tony Evans**, President, The Urban Alternative and Senior Pastor, Oak Cliff Bible Fellowship

"To know Larnelle, his quiet but engaged demeanor, his humble but confident spirit, his professional but never condescending attitude, you would never guess that he has been all over the world at some of the most prestigious events and received such an impressively wide collection of citations and awards. That's why you should not miss making the journey with him through a life that started out simply and has, by his own choice, ended up simply. It's the life of a man who loves God, cherishes his wife, adores his kids and gives thanks every day for the friends who have walked through his days. Now, I call that an amazing man."

— **Gloria Gaither**, Christian Songwriter of the Century

"What an amazing story of family, talent, mentors, and perseverance. Embracing and applauding Larnelle and Cynthia (Mitzy) has been one of the joys of my WKU presidency. They both epitomize the WKU spirit and the values we want our alumni to reflect. I knew about Larnelle's immense talent and stage presence, and I have come to know Cynthia's quiet but strong and confident leadership as a member of our governing board. Larnelle's story is one of a great American, Kentuckian, and Hilltopper (and the family which supports him) who has brought joy and faith to the lives of a multitude of fans. Well done!"

—**Gary A. Ransdell**, President of Western Kentucky University, 1997-2017

"Larnelle Harris is a name known across genres, denominations and cultures. His extraordinary vocals have surpassed all musical boundaries with what seems little effort. How wonderful that he would now be sharing his own personal story of the early struggles, the amazing opportunities and the special people that brought guidance and direction to his acclaimed legacy. This book will be one you will not want to put down until it is completed."

—**Joni Lamb**, Vice-President, Daystar Television Network

"The music of Larnelle Harris was the soundtrack of my life in the early days when I was finding my way as a Christian singer. Larnelle Harris did for me what many people did for him. He helped me to discover my voice. In reading his life story, we can see, in beautiful detail, how God's plan created a future and a hope for him. This heart-warming book confirms what we've known in our hearts all along. Larnelle Harris is not only a treasure to the church, but to the world."

— **Babbie Mason**, Award-winning singer-songwriter and author

"For more than thirty years, our families have lived life together. We have seen up-close the unwavering consistency of the man reflected in these pages. Yet in typical Larnelle fashion, he puts the focus on those who helped define him. A world-class singer, blessed with an amazing gift, yet driven by a higher call. The story he needed to tell. The story we need to hear. This is Larnelle Harris."

— **Dave Clark**, Award winning songwriter of 26 #1 songs

SHAPED NOTES

*How Ordinary People with
Extraordinary Gifts Influenced
My Life and Career*

LARNELLE HARRIS
with CHRISTINE SCHAUB

NASHVILLE

NEW YORK • MELBOURNE • VANCOUVER

SHAPED NOTES
*How Ordinary People with Extraordinary Gifts
Influenced My Life and Career*

© 2018 LARNELLE HARRIS

Published in New York, New York, by Morgan James Publishing. Morgan James is a trademark of Morgan James, LLC. www.MorganJamesPublishing.com

The Morgan James Speakers Group can bring authors to your live event. For more information or to book an event visit The Morgan James Speakers Group at www.TheMorganJamesSpeakersGroup.com.

ISBN 978-1-68350-527-3 paperback
ISBN 978-1-68350-528-0 eBook
Library of Congress Control Number: 2017905314

Cover Design by:
Rachel Lopez
www.r2cdesign.com

Interior Design by:
Bonnie Bushman
The Whole Caboodle Graphic Design

In an effort to support local communities, raise awareness and funds, Morgan James Publishing donates a percentage of all book sales for the life of each book to Habitat for Humanity Peninsula and Greater Williamsburg.

Get involved today! Visit
www.MorganJamesBuilds.com

DEDICATION

Mitzy and I have been married for a very long time and my respect and thanks for having her in my life goes far beyond what might be said in the dedication section of this or any book. She has truly been the cohesive element that has made Lonnie, Teresa and me a family. For her life-long contribution to this project, and the ongoing commitment to our future years together, I am eternally grateful and dedicate this offering to her. Every December 19th on our anniversary, I spend a good part of the day talking her into another year. I shall be doing the same in years to come.

And of course, to Noran, who was more than a booking agent to me and my family. She scheduled the first event in my over 40 years of solo concerts, and watched over me like a mother hen. She has gone on to be with the Lord and is dearly missed.

TABLE OF CONTENTS

PREFACE

I never set out in life to be extraordinarily ordinary. I may have been looked upon as just another poor black kid from the back roads of Kentucky, but then I opened my mouth and a clear soprano voice came out that made people sit up, listen, and take action.

All kinds of people involved themselves in that voice—kind souls in our little community, teachers with long reaches into higher education, movers and shakers in the music industry, and a loving, nurturing family. Each one of them held out a hand, beckoned me to take it, and said things like, "trust me" and "I think you should go for it." And when I did, I was rarely disappointed. How many times might I have given up, if not for these people? Countless. How many of them would have let me quit? None.

Even at my darkest, most frightened moments, these people, these voices kept beating the drum, reassuring me I could push through it, get around it, move past it…and none of those voices were louder than the Lord's.

I've had a lot of fun and shed a few tears writing down the memories of these people shaping direct paths and particular notes in my life's song. I hope you enjoy reading them as much as I loved remembering them.

— **Larnelle Harris**

Chapter 1

THE BEGINNING

When I was seven or eight, I was standing in the front yard on a warm, sunny day when the local police showed up, put my dad into handcuffs, and hauled him away. I don't remember a trial, but I remember seeing Mom on her knees, praying, praying…

Like most children, I didn't really understand my parents and how the first half of their lives were complex and messy, and ultimately shaped the man, the singer, the father, the son they hoped I would become.

My folks were everyday people trying to make a living for the family. There wasn't a lot of intellectual banter about philosophy or political climates or theological ideologies at the dinner table. They didn't sit me down to debate moral dilemmas. We didn't role play or engage in mock debates. They lived by a culture of example and self-determination: They felt if they created a place of love and safety for me, whatever I was going to be, I would find it.

I was deep into adulthood before I understood how they had both come from adversarial backgrounds, somehow found each other, and agreed to not live that way anymore. So, I'm starting with their story and how if they had conscientiously set out to establish a mantra for me, it would be this: "Be a good person by being in the right place, doing what you're supposed to be doing at that time." That's it. They had wisdom that comes from life experience which, in many instances, is more useful than a fistful of degrees in dealing with human frailty and success. That's what they wanted for me.

I Do!

My dad, Oscar Harris, Jr, was 23 when he married my mom, Ida "May" Dodd, age 28, on a cold Saturday in late-November 1941 in Danville, Kentucky. No one knows how they met, but Dad may have taken the 36-mile jaunt from Danville to Lexington on a church or club outing and bumped into her there. Mom was a runaway then—she'd run back to her birthplace to escape an abusive relationship that saw her married at 13 with five subsequent kids when she was just a kid herself with a third-grade education. She had left everything and everyone behind in a place called Stoneacre, West Virginia and was taken in by a lovely couple who lived with us for many years. I always knew them as my grandparents.

Mom's past made me very, very sad and very angry—not angry at her, but at the reputation she got as a runaway, leaving behind five kids. That whole time is something those kids have tried to forget, tried to get away from, because they were told their mother was wild and crazy and just looking out for herself. That wasn't the truth, but it was drilled into them. And they came looking for her anyway. Dad stood ready to become a father the moment Mom's children moved in (but my arrival some six years later was a bit of a surprise). The two girls lived with us, and the boys would stop in when they passed through. They were good siblings, searching for some answers to nullify some of those rumors. They found out their mother was a great lady, and they started coming around more and more.

White Whiskey & Donuts

During National Prohibition, Kentucky's terrain and rurality made it ideal for making moonshine. It wasn't against the law to distill liquor in the backwoods, then store it in Mason jars for personal use. But it was considered a punishable offense to "bootleg" or smuggle it to buyers in town. When Prohibition was repealed in 1933, many Kentucky counties were still "dry" and the occupation of illegally transporting and selling alcohol into dry counties flourished.

My dad was a bootlegger. And so were some other members on his side of the family, including his daddy. This was not a secret in our family—it was considered a business, and these men considered themselves businessmen, not criminals. The Harris family had a farm about 10 miles out of Danville—in bone-dry Boyle County—in a place called Persimmon Knobs, where the boys weren't required to go to school past the eighth grade. Dad worked at a filling station and as a farmhand, but couldn't join the Army and gain that structure because of issues with his feet. The one instinct in everybody is survival. To make a decent living, you revert to whatever it is you were doing or observed, and what was modeled for Dad was just this side of the law. And "outside the law" is not a place to be.

Mom was not comfortable with it, but she understood Dad was trying to make a living for his family out of a limited education and scant job opportunities. Now, Dad was not an Al Capone. He was getting by. I think if he could have made a living doing something else, he would have. But I'll tell you this: When I was a little guy, I could sell you a pint of Kentucky brew just as well as he could.

There were some rough years when circumstances forced them to be somewhere they really did not want to be. Dad was not a career criminal, and I'm certain Mom tried to pray us out of that life. We went to church, but I don't know that Dad understood what being a Christian was all about. Believe it or not, bootleggers go to church. Drug dealers and cartel kingpins go to church. That doesn't make them Christians. Mom was praying Dad into the faith…praying for a change in his life and a change in ours—a stability that doesn't come from money.

There were arguments. There were nights I heard my dad outside the front door, knocking, calling "May? May?" and she wouldn't let him in. All of this affected me greatly. I remember playing in the front yard one day with my toy six-shooters, my granddaddy's old Hudson sitting in the drive, baking in the hot sun, listening to my parents arguing in the house. They came out through the front door, Dad was holding her hard, drew his hand back to hit her, and she said, "Don't do it." I drew that cap gun, pointed it at my dad, and pulled the trigger. *Pop, pop, pop.* If that gun had been real, I would have shot him. That gun was real to me in that moment. If I could have spoken, if I could've written a treatise at that point, I would have listed all the reasons for "Why You Should Die Right Now." And you will…if you keep that up. The noise stopped Dad in his tracks and he turned and looked at me, immediately let go of Mom, then went somewhere. That's what Mom was praying about. That was a defining moment. I think that day my dad considered all the ramifications of a six-year-old kid living with a bootlegger, aiming a gun at his dad and pulling the trigger. The gun was a toy, but the frustration I was feeling was very real. As I look back on that moment, I believe for the first time he thought, *What is my kid going be like? What am I teaching?*

But the change didn't come soon enough. The law caught up to his bootlegging. We were stunned at his arrest but not surprised at the outcome, as it wasn't hidden from any of the kids that our uncle and grandfather were in prison for similar crimes.

My dad spent a year in a Kentucky prison. Mom was heartbroken, but she kept everything together. She worked as a maid and in a dry cleaner's. News in a small community spreads fast, and I'm sure my teachers knew our circumstances, knew about my dad and made certain I kept succeeding. People were very kind to Mom. During that long year, we didn't have to move out of our house, we didn't have bill collectors knocking on our door, and I don't remember wanting for anything. I'm sure there was a lot of adult business going on behind the scenes, but Mom and the community protected me.

And with all of that backdrop, she still had the strong faith that God could do exactly what He said He would. And even though He hadn't taken her out of the situation she was in, she knew He heard her and she had faith He would work it out. I know this because I was there on my knees beside her. I didn't understand everything she was saying. I was a little guy. But I knew she was down on her knees beside the bed, praying for Dad. I didn't have to understand the words or know how many times she prayed, but I, too, believed God was hearing her. I believe now that prison was part and parcel of God answering Mom's prayer. We may think prison can't be a part of prayer. Listen, pain is a part of God's plan for our lives. It refines us. So Mom would pray and she would expect results—she had a childlike faith.

A year later, Dad completed his sentence, walked out of prison and into a new life. When he got out, he had a trade. He had learned to bake. Dad's change of direction is probably as much responsible for my not going to prison as anything else in my life. At Burke's Bakery, what Dad modeled in front of me was not a trade where you're always looking over your shoulder, but an art of taking donuts out of the sugar and hanging them up…and the sugar's dripping down and old man Burke and the rest of the staff are hanging around, having office relationships. My dad's in a white cap and apron and I'm eating a hot donut and… my dad made that! And pecan pie…my dad made that! That's a big difference from, "My dad will sell you a pint." I will always be grateful to Mr. Burke for giving dad a job and a second chance.

Dad took his natural entrepreneurial spirit and, once he found an outlet for the same risk he took being outside the law, it became positive. He was finally doing something he was very proud of that he could see and was successful. He was known throughout town for his rolls and fruitcakes. He began to buy property and turn it into rental income. He bought a farm and began to raise livestock. It was honest, good work. It was something he created to take care of his family.

I believe our life was one way, then it became another when my parents made a conscious decision to make a better life for all of us. I saw them struggling to figure out who they were going to be, day to day. Had I not heard or seen some of those instances where I knew something was amiss—the arguments, the late-night knocking..."May? May?"...those times when men are trying to figure out what being a man is supposed to look like... Had I not been there when Mom was on her knees, praying like a warrior, or lived through that dark day of arrest and year when Dad went away... Had I not tasted that donut my dad, the baker, had made... I probably would have just accepted who my dad was. This little boy needed to see all those situations unfold in real time, because events shape your life.

There's a dignity in living through life's challenges, then coming out on the other side. We found that dignity. I believe Dad learned respect for Mom before he learned it for himself. He really loved her, and I was so overjoyed by the man he was becoming. And then I discovered my dad was a man I could respect.

Becoming a Man

Dad and I started to talk more man-to-man and we developed a different kind of relationship. I saw him taking pride in his son. There's nothing a kid needs more than to know his mother and father are proud of him. When I sang in church, neither one of them said, "He's gonna be famous!" They just affirmed it was the right thing to do and I did it well. I think they dreamed I would be something, but they didn't know what or how to get there necessarily. What they did was create a place, make it as safe as they could, then turn me loose. They probably hoped when I bumped up against a wall I wouldn't get hurt too badly. But they might have hoped for a little pain, otherwise I would never know what I could overcome.

A lot of their early advice centered on learning to be careful, because this is a black-and-white world. Danville, like a lot of small towns in Kentucky, was mainly segregated. I didn't spend a lot of time with white kids growing up, although I made friends with a little girl in a house Mom cleaned, and sometimes played with the son of a diamond broker who was actively trying to break down racial barriers with his son.

What my parents advised would antagonize me. Mom and I would be walking downtown, she would be holding my hand and some guy would try to walk over us. And I wouldn't move. I was developing some unhealthy anger. I think every kid goes through that for various reasons, but my parents preached caution: "Know where you are. Understand where you are. Know what side of town you're on. Be careful." I didn't grow up with a lot of hate. My parents didn't teach me hate. Our church didn't teach me hate. School leaders didn't teach me hate. But we all learned caution. And I still have it.

Mom was naturally a little suspicious, and that's how her strictness and protective instincts kicked in. We had our rounds—"One of these days," I told her, "I'm gonna get out of here!" She had her way of dealing with me and when she made up her mind that was pretty much how it was going to be. For instance: One of the things I always wanted to do, because I could hear it from my bedroom window, was go to Swingland. That was where everybody went to dance in a big old barn. But Mom forbade me to go. When I started messing with the guitar, some friends of mine all played guitars and I would go to their house and mess around with them. I could hear them playing at Swingland! So I determined I would sneak off and go. I went and stood in that barn a few minutes and thought, This is nothing. Of course, when you aren't allowed to go somewhere and go anyway, you feel a little angst or a little exhilaration. I felt like I was in the wrong place, at the wrong time, and I really didn't belong there. Mom was right, but I had to find that out for myself. My parents got smarter as I got older. So I didn't give them a lot trouble. I respected them.

I am not certain of the dynamics, but I remember meeting my paternal grandparents for the first time when I was very young, Looking back now, there seemed to be a level of tension in the family. Maybe it was some over-caution on my parent's part. Word on the street was my grandfather was sent to prison for killing a man over a nickel crap game. So, once my parents moved to Danville, we didn't go visit them much, but my aunt would come to visit with her newborn. I adored her and my little cousin. She lived, as she says, "across the track," but I always considered her a little "uptown"—prim, proper, and elegant. "Your mom and dad were very protective," she told me. "So they kept you close. We were across the track." Well, all of Danville was a "track." If Aunt Willie and Melvin were across the track, then surely we were too!

Because my parents lived out their faith and drastically improved their lives, our family tree changed forever. My grandfather had lived out a good part of his life in prison. My father had served time. But I never did. And my son didn't. A long-standing pattern had finally been broken in our family.

Chapter 2
FINDING MY VOICE

Every child needs a tour guide—someone who volunteers to unselfishly and persistently stay on the case, turn on the light and keep shining it, set the example of successful, purposeful living. These guides must be fearless, encouraging, passionate, patient, intuitive, experimental, opportunistic.

I had a series of tour guides throughout my educational and formative years who were all these things and more. I didn't recognize them at the time…I was just making my way through life, day by day. I had no long-term goals, no particular ambitions. The future was abstract to me, but not to them. They nudged me along, little by little, shaping me into the man I am today. Here are their stories.

Singing for Tea

Miss Georgia Donehy was probably my first promoter. Single all her life, she dedicated her time and energy toward church music, and particularly those who were part of the First Baptist Church in Danville, Kentucky. She played piano and organ, accompanied the choir and soloists, and gave piano lessons to every kid in town, whether they wanted them or not.

I didn't want them, but my mother wanted me to want them, so I had to want them. During my mother's quest to find the virtuoso spilling out of my tiny, reluctant fingers, Miss Georgie (as we all called her) discovered I could sing…soprano. And that's where it all started—not the discovery of a singing phenomenon, but the beginning of a series of people God would put in my path to help me find my real voice.

I guess I was a little odd-sounding to the folks at our church. Most of us kids had never heard a boy soprano or the Vienna Boys Choir. But Miss Georgie had. Before I knew it, I was performing as a church soloist, nine years old, singing famous church hymns like "How Great Thou Art" and "The Lord's Prayer." The church ladies would just cry when I would hit those high notes. She would take me to sing at the local Catholic Church, and I remember being up in the choir loft in the back of the church, singing "Twelve Gates to the City," later made popular by singers like Carly Simon and Joan Baez. I would have to put on my best clothes and be the entertainment at ladies' teas. Small groups of five or 10 or 15 ladies would sit in sort of a book club circle, nibbling finger foods, and Miss Georgie would introduce me with "How Great Thou Art," my soprano voice soaring.

These were not things I always wanted to do as a kid. I didn't really grasp the significance of these performances. And sometimes Miss Georgie got on my bad side, like the time she told my mother I shouldn't try out for the Little League football team because the dust would hurt my voice! But I've long since realized something special was happening. God used those events as a preview of how I was to serve Him—to use music to tell others about His great love.

Miss Georgie understood the significance—she knew what was going on behind the scenes. She did her best to get together as many people as possible to hear a little boy sing from his heart about the heart of God. She picked up music and put it right into my hands.

I hope every town has a Miss Georgia Donehy.

Listening Forward

While the ladies were weeping at my high notes, my peers were laughing. It's not easy being a boy soprano in an all-black school in a small town in Kentucky.

I dodged a lot of teasing at the Bate School—a segregated one-room shanty "common school" started in 1868 with six students and one teacher that John W. Bate transformed into an accredited standard school with 20 rooms, 600 students and 15 teachers. So many educators from that fine school were more than teachers. They were look-outs. They were advisers, eyeing the future, creating intentional plans of action, keeping us listening forward, working to equip us with the knowledge and skills that would help us throughout our lives to be productive human beings. They were always trying to find a way to turn on a light somewhere, to show us what was out there, outside Danville, Kentucky. They were not just there to make sure we made it to the next grade.

Critical to my future success were Miss Margaret Helm—my first-grade teacher and woman of my dreams (demanding and encouraging), Miss Dale—my second-grade teacher and elementary choir leader (patient and clever), Miss Fisher—librarian and community leader (bold and ground-breaking), and Mr. Summers—principal, leader, life-changer.

Mr. Summers laid down the law and insisted we follow it…and used the paddle to back it up. He spent much of his time, as far as I could see, just keeping us in line. As a student, you didn't want to draw any kind of attention that was going to require his "input." But due to my boy-soprano status, I was drawing a lot of attention from my peers, most of it in the form of teasing.

One day in the lunch line I got into a shoving match with another boy—probably about this voice I had been "blessed with"—when Mr. Summers suddenly appeared out of nowhere. It was off to the principal's office for both of us. I viewed Mr. Summers as a guy with a paddle who wasn't shy about using it, so I sat in the hall, anxiously awaiting my turn to get my share of the licks for the shoving crime. I knew full well if I did get a spanking—though my home was without a telephone or other means of immediate communication—my dad would somehow find out about it, meet me halfway home, and when we got home, well… you know.

My turn came. I walked down what seemed like an endless amount of steps into his dungeon den of an office. The infamous paddle was sitting in just the right position on his desk to be grabbed easily and quickly. It was evident he'd done this a few times. He said something to me, but my thoughts were not on his words. And the next thing I knew, he—"Bub" Summers, a name nobody dared call him to his face—started singing. I was stunned. We feared this guy. Nobody, but nobody, wanted to be in his crosshairs. And he was singing! The thought of getting a spanking still loomed, but now I just listened. Deep within him, somewhere, came a high, clear baritone voice...rich and beautiful.

He was sending me a message: It's okay to be different. Don't sweat it. Embrace it.

Mr. Summers turned on a light. From that point on, much less of my existence hinged on those "perceived" negative things my peers said. From that point on, it was easier to sing.

The Greatest Profession

Miss Helen Fisher Frye sat me down in the library one day in my freshman year and said, "Listen—we're going to start looking for a trade school for you because I'm not certain you're college material." She said it out of love. She knew my family and circumstances, and she wanted to encourage me to begin thinking about my plans beyond high school. She had my best interests at heart, and she was trying to guide me as best she knew how. She was trying to prepare me for the harsh realities of the real world.

Only later in life did I understand Miss Fisher and many of the Bate School teachers had been born and raised right in Danville, Kentucky, in a period of tremendous racial tension. During those tumultuous years, Bate School would have been one of only a few schools available to black kids. In fact, Miss Fisher used to drive Mr. Bate—son of slaves—to various educational seminars and conferences around Kentucky. Miss Fisher bore a lot of the hate and obstacles and brunt of discrimination that was totally unfair to begin with.

By the time I entered Bate, the school was overcrowded, understaffed and underfunded. But we didn't notice. We didn't understand the struggle, the extreme lengths our teachers had gone to in order to get a bachelor's degree so they could give back to the black community and make our lives better. This was not a career or profession or calling just handed to them. It was a fight. It was a mission to fix a wrong, to right the ship, to provide a quality education to us from an unselfish point of view.

She took that experience and taught us to strive, to hope. She wanted us to be realistic about how harsh and unjust the real world could be. With a hard-won BA in elementary education and two master degrees in secondary education and library science, she was highly capable and very well prepared to lead us. She used to say, "I love teaching—not subjects, but people."

I so appreciate the selflessness of Miss Fisher and the Bate School staff for speaking into my life. They really loved and cared for us and wanted us to succeed, and did everything in their power to make it so.

Learning to Jam

Mr. William Cherry was a fine man and band director who welcomed me into the Bate School Band as a saxophone player. He gave me limited lessons on fingering and notes, and figuring out the rest was sort of up to me. Miss Georgie's piano lessons had provided a great background for understanding chord structure and visualizing music, and I struggled along with notes and scales and tried to put on a good show for Mr. Cherry.

And then he needed some drummers. So I picked up the drums and started playing them in the marching band in my sophomore year. I was self-taught at that time and proudly gave my best on the field and in parades. And then every once in a while, I would join Mr. Cherry at a gig in Lexington. See, he wasn't just a band director, he played the organ. This was the era of The Incredible Jimmy Smith—jazz organist and improviser, and Jimmy McGriff—hard bop and soul-jazz organist, (both popularized the Hammond B-3 electric organ), and Mr. Cherry was like one of them. He needed a drummer at these performances and chose me! We had a great relationship and I appreciate everything he taught me.

Then, the summer before my junior year, Bate High School consolidated with Danville High School, and I was introduced to a band director who saw even more potential in me.

I still remember the first summer day the combined band students were gathered in the band room, talking, socializing, making a little noise, when somebody ran into the room and said, "Here he comes! Here he comes!" And into the hushed room walked McCauley (Mac) Arthur. He was all business, very somber, very matter-of-fact, giving us a little orientation of what he expected. We wouldn't be playing around under the direction of Mac Arthur. Being in his band was going to be an intense experience.

Next thing I knew, we were off to band camp at Eastern Kentucky University, on the tarmac in the hot sun, marching and getting into shape for the school year's activities. Occasionally, someone would fall faint and Mac and the student leaders would shout, "Keep going! Do not stop!" It was tough! This was all new to me—band camp (which we didn't have at Bate School) and music rehearsals where Mac passed out music, gave the downbeat, and everyone started to play. They were sight-reading the music! I flashed back to Miss Georgie, who sight-read like a fiend. Finally, *finally*, I had a great desire to pull out a piece of music, read it, and play it—not by ear, guessing, working it out. But to actually read it.

Maybe because of the intense competition in that band, I had a desire to outdo the other drummers, to excel. I started really paying attention, figuring out beats and rests, counting. In my senior year, I was good enough to become a leader in the drum section, but I was still reading on a basic level and I wanted to learn more. Enter Mac.

Mac approached me with an idea: drum lessons. He asked me, "If I get you a drum teacher, will you practice?" I said, "Sure!" So he gave me a music theory book and found a drum student at Centre College in Danville to teach me the 26 rudiments—proper sticking of the rhythms on the page, akin to scales or etudes on the piano. There's a hard way and an easy way to do it, a right way to get the proper accents and rolls. I had very good hands. I just needed to learn the proper mechanics. The student-teacher showed me rudiments and how to read them, and I took one of the drums home from school and practiced all the time in the house.

About that time, my dad suddenly needed an office out back. He built a little shed behind the house that accommodated an office for his coal business—and allowed me to practice my drums. Peace and quiet in the house, hours and hours of noisy practicing in the shed. Win-win.

Understanding the rudiments and sticking techniques helped me play the drum solos my teacher would find and give me to rehearse. He would give me one solo out of the book, and I would do half the book. And then I would do all of the book. And then I would go back and do the whole book again. I went through everything he had, hundreds of times. Some of the solos were quite difficult and I had to practice and work out those passages as I would with any instrument. About a month into the lessons, the teacher said, "There's nothing else I can teach you." He didn't realize how badly I had wanted to play and be able to read something set in front of me...and be good at it! And now I could read! The band music was incredibly easy compared to the rudimental solos, and that's when I became a real asset to the marching band.

This was just the first of the tremendous educational gifts from Mac.

About that time, Mac approached me with another important question: "What are you going to do with your life?" I had no idea, but I had this musical talent. He had heard me sing in concert band and choir, chorus and musicals like *H.M.S. Pinafore*, and he had watched my progression to section leader in the band, so he knew my capabilities. He talked to my parents—who knew nothing about applying for higher education—and suddenly I was on my way to a couple of colleges to audition for music scholarships. He drove me to Eastern Kentucky University in Richmond where I interviewed with the music faculty to indifferent results. Then he drove me to his alma mater, Western Kentucky University in Bowling Green, where I auditioned with drums and voice for instrumental teacher/conductor Dr. Howard Carpenter and voice teacher Ohm Pauli. I was offered a full scholarship in vocal and percussion to WKU, which meant I would be in practically every music program they had. And that was OK with me because I was hungry…hungry to learn.

Mac guided that ship with the kind of intensity only present in teachers with a heart for their students' futures, exactly like the kinds of teachers I had at Bate. He didn't just tell me to take lessons…he found a teacher. He didn't just tell me to further my education…he drove me to auditions. And when I got that scholarship, he didn't just slap me on the back and say, "Good luck!" He helped me apply for a dorm and schooled me on the enrollment process. He did it all—it was his idea. I simply followed along and got caught up in his excitement. And I'll be forever thankful for those lifelong gifts from McCauley "Mac" Arthur.

Becoming a Hilltopper

As a scholarship student, I was very serious about my musical training. But no one was more serious, more all-business than my voice teacher, Mr. Ohm Pauli. He'd arranged for my scholarship, so he took it personally to help me retain it. Like I had with the drums, I had winged singing without formal training for years and it was time to get into the rudiments.

I learned about the four properties of tone, how to position the pitch of my voice, the "Do-Re-Mi" series of notes in the scale. And within all of that was the element of reading—that essential skill Miss Georgia had tried so hard to instill in me, but I had rejected because I was a kid and took every short-cut I could.

Mr. Pauli also directed the Western Choir and Madrigal Singers, and retired from WKU as a national-class vocal educator. He was a great teacher and noted, "I have probably had more good students than I have deserved." He was my only voice instructor at WKU and I owe much of my vocal skill to him. It was David "Doc" Livingston who added the enthusiasm and pizzazz to my college musical training. I got to Western in 1965—Doc's first year of being band director. And that's what I knew about him: band director and arranger who put together the programs for Homecoming and football games.

Then one day, he sat down at the piano and started playing. And you know the famous line from the old E.F. Hutton commercial: "When E.F. Hutton talks, people listen"? That's exactly what happened. Doc played notes and chords that brought together all the composition classes, all the music theory, all the nuances of music together in one package with an ingredient missing a lot of times: passion. As he played and improvised and hit notes I'm certain he didn't know were coming, it all came together. He had that little bit of "soul" that makes music more than just a piece, makes it something that stirs you, moves you. I remember thinking as I sat there and listened: *Who is this guy? Who is this?*

He'd sat down at the piano as Mr. Livingston, band director. But when he finished that piece, he emerged to me as David "Doc" Livingston—the man with the illustrative music career in the Army, the top jazz performer on saxophone, clarinet and piano who took multiple overseas tours with Billy Vaughn's Hollywood Orchestra, who performed with jazz greats Louis Armstrong and Dave Brubeck. I mean, he was a *musician*. And I had the privilege to learn from him!

And then he took his budding musicians up another notch by working with Dr. Howard Carpenter, head of the WKU Music Department, to put together a group of handpicked students for a variety show band called Gemini 15. Eleven college girls and four guys got together to play Doc's big band arrangements for campus and high school concerts, then picked up a sponsorship from the National Music Council to do a United Services Organization (USO) tour. Over a whirlwind five weeks, Gemini 15 visited military bases in Germany, South America, the Bahamas, and even Guantanamo Bay, entertaining soldiers with jazz numbers, ballads and folk songs. I played drums and John Carpenter (yes—*that* John Carpenter of scary movie "Halloween" fame) played bass, and the girls sang in a chorus line…and the military boys felt a little less homesick. That tour was my first little taste of a musician's life on the road.

One of my favorite Doc arrangements was "Georgia On My Mind." I remember sitting at the drums, singing it in one of our concerts at Van Meter Auditorium at WKU. My girlfriend and future wife, Mitzy, happened to be at that concert and I think it was from there she made the proclamation: "I'm gonna have this guy sing to me all my life." And that was the power behind Doc's music. It was more than soulful chords and beautiful arrangements. It was pure passion.

WKU's motto is: "The Spirit Makes the Master." To me, that statement is akin to putting yourself in a place and in a situation where you can grow in your profession, where you can grow as a person, where your vision is more than just making a grade, but wanting to know, and studying hard and striving to make the world a better place by mastering all the processes availed to you. And to adopt the spirit that causes you to innately want to pass along what you've learned and gained and gleaned.

We're called "Hilltoppers" because of that spirit. The spirit makes the master, and that spirit makes a Topper. For me, Doc Livingston exemplified that spirit, and he will always be a Topper.

These educators who've unselfishly spoken into my life—from Miss Georgie's persistence to the Bate School teachers' love and care, from Mr. Cherry's band invitation to Mac's determination at DHS to stand in my path and take an interest, from Mr. Pauli's scholarship offer and diligent instruction to Doc's brilliance—the progression seems so planned it could not have been by accident, could not have been simply another big bang theory.

I have no doubt God had His hand on my life, and I think He has His hand on all of our lives. He'll use any of us, if we allow ourselves to be used by Him. If you look back on how you got where you ended up, as I've had the opportunity to do, you too will discover it can't possibly have been an accident. It was God's plan all along.

Chapter 3

GROWING UP
ON THE ROAD

Before Roger Breland's contemporary Christian group Truth, before Cam Floria's Continentals and Derric Johnson's ReGeneration ensemble, there was Thurlow Spurr and his groundbreaking traveling gospel group called The Spurrlows. And I got my first taste of being a full-time musician on the road with them.

It was the summer of 1969, I was 22, fresh out of college and looking for an adventure. As many of these kinds of adventures happened, I knew a bass player who knew a band leader who needed a drummer. And I was a drummer. I was a *serious* drummer. I had spent hours and hours in the college practice rooms, listening to and emulating big band drummers like Buddy Rich, and it was my dream, my goal to be a famous drummer.

So I got invited to audition for The Spurrlows up in Ypsilanti, Michigan at Eastern Michigan University. Those practice hours must have paid off because I was immediately called to be part of a group I had never seen or even heard! In Danville, we never had Christian singing groups come to our church, and in college I was only around the groups existing there. Before I knew it, I was in rehearsal camp at Baker College in Owosso, Michigan, hanging out with Christian kids—some college grads, some taking off a semester or two—from all over the country and all denominations (Lutherans, Episcopalians, Baptists, Methodists) creating smooth harmonies in the Fred Waring tradition and playing modern arrangements to hymns, traditional songs, and top-40 hits. It was magical.

The relentless nine-month road trip was less magical, but it instilled a traveling work ethic in me I could only have learned in the actual doing.

Let's Put on a Show

A typical day for the Spurrlows involved 20 or more of us piling into a caravan of cars, station wagons and a tractor-trailer, driving to an area high school, pulling out all the sound and lighting equipment, sets, instruments, music, bandstands, stage decorations, props and costumes for a 30- or 45- or 60-minute concert, setting it up in about 15 minutes, and taking the stage...sometimes by 8:00 AM. Then we would tear it all down, put it all back in the truck, go to another school, set up, perform, tear down. Sometimes we did two or three assemblies a day. We traveled more than 250,000 miles, performed about 600 concerts, and entertained a million people each season. It was a lot of work and the traveling hit me hard. This was *on the road*. It was tough, but I learned so much that prepared me for a career I hadn't even dreamed of pursuing.

My group was sponsored by Chrysler Corporation, so in the midst of our "Music for Modern Americans" show, we would emphasize driving safety and the school's Driver Education Program. We played games, performed skits, wowed, amused and tried to relate to kids our age in their home setting. Our set lists included songs like George Harrison's "My Sweet Lord," The Hollies' "He Ain't Heavy, He's My Brother," "Day By Day" from the musical *Godspell*, some Carole King hits, songs by Neil Diamond, and a patriotic package. We could get away with doing songs that had "Lord" in them when they were popular on the radio. We tried to be very current in many musical genres and had about a two-hour repertoire. The aim was to do things that related to the kids, things they were already listening to. And you know what? It worked.

We had a moment toward the end of those assemblies where we would ask, "Would you like to hear another song before you go back to class?" There was always a resounding, "Yes!" So we would sing one more, then start to strike the set. A lot of times the school principals would have some of the guys help us—sort of fulfilling their dreams as roadies helping a big rock band. And sometimes kids would stay behind and just chat with us. I hope during those times we were people of character who treated the kids with respect. I found out over the years that's when most of the impression is made—when the stage is bare, when you have the opportunity to just be around people and listen, maybe even offer a word of encouragement. I'm always amazed at how that is the thing remembered. It's not the great concert. It's not the high notes. It's when I stopped for a moment, took time to care and be attentive. That's where the real ministry happens.

Whenever possible, we would invite these kids to our evening gospel concert at a church or church-sponsored function in the same city. In that day, unlike now, you could speak about God and Christ and church in schools. They'd go home and tell their parents about the evening concert, and word would spread, and we would have a great crowd for a very different message.

At night, independent of the Chrysler Corporation, we would set up on the church stage and present "Splendor of Sacred Song." Some of the songs were big production numbers brought in by Otis Skillings—who was a fine arranger and conductor, Stan Morse—an arranger, fine trombone player, and winner of Ted Mack's Original Amateur Hour (an early televised talent show with winners like Gladys Knight and Tanya Tucker) and Darrell Rodman—arranger, pianist and trumpeter. They orchestrated hymns and spirituals that capitalized on the individual talents in the group, like a high soprano who sang a beautiful arrangement of "Wayfaring Stranger." There were some very talented people in the Spurrlows.

A lot of church-goers were suspect of the whole idea of "contemporary Christian" music. They didn't want drums or electric guitars or pop arrangements. Sometimes we had to sneak into the evening venue and get the drums set up early, so if somebody came in and said, "We don't have drums in this church…" it was just too much trouble to tear it all down. So, the church would agree to accept drums *just for tonight*. Quite often, our evening program was the first taste churches had of anything sounding like modern Christian music. We came in, gave a quality, dynamic performance, and people were suddenly seeing the effect it had on their youth.

After this concert, we would invite attendees to receive Christ. With follow-up designed by the Spurrlow organization, we would use a pamphlet called "The Four Spiritual Laws" from Campus Crusades for Christ to witness and talk to kids. I was little more than a kid myself, but I knew all about the angst and pain and confusion that would cause kids to break down in tears when I offered to lead them in a prayer of repentance. I believe we were able to do our little bit to help some of those hurting kids who, in turn, might help other kids with the same issues. We would always try to steer them into a good church or any place with good youth programs, caring pastors and kind teachers to help them find answers they desperately needed to thrive.

Some of the kids received the message of Christ and were very thankful, and some walked away. But at least the seed was planted. It was our hope and prayer some of those kids went on to be strong Christian leaders. As a kid myself, I wasn't totally aware of the impact of receiving Christ, although I really believed Christ was the answer. And I did leave some concerts thinking, *I did something really important here.*

Stan Morse was the Spurrlows' point person for the audition camp. He was a terrific musician and a very sensitive, caring person. As I listened to the testimonies of kids auditioning with me, I wondered why my own testimony didn't sound like any of theirs. I was 12 years old when I went down to the altar of our church in Danville. The pastor asked me how I felt and I told him I felt just fine—which he took to mean I was saved and understood all that entailed. I think many of us do that as kids, and I believe God accepts and honors our decisions at any age, keeping us in a place of security until we grow into maturity, learning the tenants of our faith and why we believe them.

As I chatted with Stan that summer of '69, he helped guide me into solidifying my relationship with Christ. I will forever be grateful for the counsel he gave me, as well as his genuine concern for my salvation and my walk with the Lord.

Breaking Out

I was happily drumming in the Spurrlows' back-up band when Otis Skilling brought in an arrangement of "Oh Happy Day"—a hit song all over the radio by the Edwin Hawkins Singers. The arrangers were trying out different soloists for it and two of my band mates—trumpeter Dorman and bass player James—suggested I give it a shot. Well, everybody was a little surprised because up to that point, I hadn't sung a note for them! But Dorman and James graduated from WKU with me and knew I sang and said, "Listen—sing this for Otis." So I got up there and sang, "Oh happy day…oh happy day…when Jesus washed… my sins away."

That was it, and suddenly I was singing that song and playing the drums at the same time. After a few concerts, the arrangers felt like I needed to get up from the drums and finish the song out front. So with a little stagecraft and help from another drummer in the group, I slipped out from behind the drum set, he slipped in, and I finished the song standing up front. That little maneuver was always a hit.

After that, the arrangers started looking for other songs for me. Darrell had a way of putting chords together that was very modern, yet very rich. He did a beautiful *Porgy and Bess*-style arrangement for "I Want to Be More Like Jesus"—a song I sang as a child. His arrangements just touched me…made my heart move.

At that time, the Spurrlows were a great shot in the arm for young Christian musicians who wanted to sing and play great music, but didn't necessarily want to be in clubs or someplace where their testimonies would be compromised. This was an outlet to make great music and be part of a great Christian group traveling around the country. It was such a romantic thought, that kind of yearning to take a year off and be a missionary in the States, be part of a group playing great music for kids, then witness and minister to them.

And I am most appreciative that at a time in my life when I needed a place to be, to play, to grow and to flourish, Thurlow Spurr invited me into his group.

Changing Gears

Since my contract with the Spurrlows was good for nine months during the school year, I was off the road for the summer. This was when new singers and instrumentalists were put through a series of auditions, then rehearsals with former Spurrlows who were invited back for another contract period starting in September. I opted to return in 1970, and then in the summer of 1971, I was offered the opportunity to do something a little different.

First Gear was created from the instrumentalists who were playing for the Spurrlows band. And we liked to rock. We were seven guys with a funky jazz-rock sound featuring Tommy Wells and me on the drums, Russ Gregory on guitar, Rick Brunermer on the saxophone, Don Perry on the trombone, Randy Hammel on the organ, and Ken Cooley on bass. All of us could sing. Most of us, including Thurlow, were looking to make First Gear something that could compete in a national market, on a national scale. So we split the Gear from being part of the Spurrlows band and started working toward that end, doing concerts on our own.

We did high school assemblies as sort of a Chicago/Rare Earth/ Blood, Sweat & Tears kind of sound, but our musical style and set list didn't work in churches at night. And since many of us were married by that time and needed to keep working when schools were on break, we started performing in clubs. During the day, we worked on our sound, writing our own original songs and refining popular tunes, like Carole King's "I Feel the Earth Move" and Jerry Jeff Walker's "Mr. Bojangles."

We hit the clubs at night and played the popular songs of the day. People danced, had their hands in the air, came right up to the speakers and rocked out. It was extremely exciting and electric.

We cut a self-titled album with Myrrh Records in 1972 and kept on rocking. But it was still a "missionary" endeavor for low pay, so we really needed to work year-round. We didn't have to move around all the time, so we could rehearse and refine, and we really had a good time playing together.

But there was a darker side to the club scene...a different lifestyle. We were interested in music and trying to make something of our group, but that nightlife began to pull at us. We developed relationships with guys and gals who were after something different. And it yanked, it pulled and challenged my faith. I was developing questions about my beliefs and about my Christian lifestyle. The Bible says, "Taste and see that the Lord is good." Well, I tasted the world and it was sweet in my mouth, but when it got to my stomach, it soured. My propensity to run to dark places—and sometimes, the darker the better—had nothing to do with First Gear. There were no bad kids in the Gear. The darkness was just there, and I could choose it or not.

We cut another album in 1974, titled *Caution! Steep Hill, Use First Gear*, but I was on my way out. There weren't a lot of places at that time where talented Christian guys could play a different kind of music—a style our band could not have played in church. The Gear could possibly have been one of those great Christian rock bands which do very well now. But not at that time in church music.

By the summer of 1974, I opted out of First Gear and life in the clubs. And that meant leaving people I really cared about, music I really cared about. It was not an easy thing for me to do. There was a pull for me to return to live my life by a barometer established in my family, in my formative years. I came to a place every Christian has to discover: choosing to follow Jesus' lead, discovering I liked being in the arms of my Lord and concentrating all of my efforts on growing in Him. When I turned and really began to follow the Lord at that time of my life, He led me to where He wanted me to go.

Gloria Gaither once said something I go back to often: "Sometimes you've gotta say 'no' to something in order to say 'yes' to something higher." So I said, "no." I didn't say "no" to the club scene to say "yes" to my career or the Grammys, the Doves, or the places I've traveled. I said "yes" to being a Christian, being His, being called by His name. That's more important than being part of anything the world has to offer.

Chapter 4

LIFE WITH MITZY

I bumped into Miss Cynthia Diana Sloan at WKU on the bleachers in Diddle Arena. Both of us arrived with little time to prepare for the first year of college, so we began to help each other with the registration and orientation process. She seemed to know what she was doing—she's always had that know-how confidence—so I charmed her into helping me. And then I charmed her into walking around the concourse. And then I charmed her into being my friend. The best move I have ever made.

We ran around with the same circle of friends—some from my hometown of Danville, some from her hometown of Louisville. After that first year, I was playing drums with Doc in supper clubs around town, trying to make some extra money, and didn't go home on the weekends. My friend Tim, who was from Danville and on the WKU track team, had this great idea of finding a girl and taking her to a movie and dinner. So one weekend, we convinced Cynthia to go with us, took off in my old red Rambler, and she got a taste of what hanging out with a musician was like.

I made certain I didn't get sent home that first year. I studied hard to stay in school and keep my scholarship. But I made some of my best grades—as did Mitzy—when we officially became a couple. We played hard and studied hard together. In fact, that was the first year I made the "Who's Who" list of college students.

Singing for my Future

Freshman year involved a lot of "light dating"—going out in groups, pairing up, meeting other interesting people, dating them. We were just kids, learning what it was like to spend quality time with others. I had recently come off a hometown relationship with a girl who dumped me for another guy at her college, so I was ready to explore. Then one night in a grill across from my dorm in North Hall, Cynthia started talking about relationships. "When I'm dating a guy, I just like to be with him," she said. "I like to be where they are, and be a part of what they're doing and have them be part of what I'm doing." Well, that impressed me! And I started thinking very seriously about what a relationship with this remarkable woman might be like.

Shortly after that, Gemini 15 got together and performed our first concert for WKU students. Cynthia was in the audience and, I didn't know it then, but I sealed the deal with a rendition of "Georgia On My Mind," an arrangement done by Doc Livingston. She says she probably would've married Ray Charles if she could have, but she thought I was really good as a substitute. She began to think a long-term relationship with a singer/drummer might just work for her.

STANDING, l-r: James Ownby, David Livingston, Director, Rosemary Gohagen; 2nd Row: Loraelle Harris, Karen Cone, Anita Mills, Jane Drennon, Charlotte Duncan, Carla Bratcher; 1st Row, Lft. to rt: Sara Lawrence, Robbie Day, Jamie Carlyle, Brenda Falsey, Karen Hubbard.

GEMINI 15

I started playing some gigs in Bowling Green and Louisville with Doc, and sometimes she'd get dressed up and go with me to the supper clubs on an uptown date. It wasn't long before I started making trips to Louisville to visit her family. I found out the name "Cynthia" was just a formality for the Sloans, and that everybody called her what her daddy nicknamed her: "Mitzy." In fact, virtually no one in her family went by their given name! Conversations might include someone named "Booger" or "Dump" or "Spooky" or "Splink." I might be talking to Aunt Bernee—who was really Vernita, or Aunt Rit—who was really Maddie. We were married for years when I realized the "Aunt Pete" everyone referred to in conversation was really Mitzy's mama—who'd always been Mrs. Sloan or Louise to me!

We had our share of rocky times in college, but we made it through intact as a couple. When we graduated in 1969, I went on the road with the Spurrlows and Mitzy went to work teaching school. She bought a brand-new Volkswagen Bug, lived at home, and we both saved up a little money. So imagine her parents' concerns when a traveling musician, making about $17 a week, started talking about marrying their daughter…and taking her on the road with him! I remember talking to her daddy, trying to explain to a guy who's got rough hands from working on the railroad all his life about how our lives are "out there somewhere," that "God's got a plan for us." Ah, romance.

The biggest problem they had was Mitzy actually quitting her job. The only way their generation left a job was if they were fired or the position was terminated. You just didn't walk away, in their minds. But that's what she did. We got married in December of 1971, she paid off her car loan, we honeymooned in Niagara Falls, packed up our stuff into a rental car and headed to St. Louis for the next leg of the tour.

First Gear was an all-guy band with only one other woman on the tour. And Mitzy loved it. The guys took her in like a little sister, particularly our road manager, Keith. Her job was to manage the record and memorabilia sales, count the earnings, keep track of product, and make bank deposits the next day. We were on the road more than nine months out of the year. We didn't have a house, our lodging and meals were paid for, we stayed in an interesting mix of really nice and really bad hotels. It was a fascinating and wild time in our post-graduate lives, and we really loved it for a while.

We found out our son Lonnie (my childhood moniker) was on his way in March of 1974. We went home in April to tell our parents and drop off Mitzy, then I was back on the road. But I knew I was done with the club scene, and some of the other guys were as well. And 30 days later, I was home.

Losing My Voice

That July, it hit us—a baby's coming! We need a house! We hadn't had any stable housing before, so we started looking around Mama Sloan's neighborhood. And lo and behold, there it was—a little house with a fenced-in back yard not five minutes from Grandma. And then we looked at the cost of the house and we thought, *This house is in the thousands. We don't have thousands!* The payments would be $120 a month and we thought, *We don't know how we're going to make it.*

Our lives were in an uproar, a baby was on the way, and I had just quit my job with First Gear. Unlike our parents, I had actually quit a job. I left. I felt I had to leave…I was going to die there. I was going to have to die someday, but I was determined it wouldn't be in a club in a rough neighborhood behind a drum set or playing a saxophone. And on top of all that, I was losing my voice.

On the road with the Spurrlows and then in First Gear, I was singing sometimes two or three times a day in high school assemblies. That was hard work. At night in the loud, smoke-filled clubs, I was rocking out with the Gear, singing over guitars and drums. My endurance went to nothing and there was a sort of cloud over my voice. I had just sung myself out. After two or three days' rest, I would feel fine and get back out there, and a couple of hours later I would be right back to having trouble.

I went to doctors in various parts of the country and the diagnosis was the same: swollen vocal folds with formation of vocal cord nodules. A nodule is a mass of tissue that grows on the vocal chords. That mass can reduce or obstruct the ability to speak…and sing. I had all the symptoms: hoarseness, pain, vocal breaks, reduced vocal range. A speech pathologist discovered my voice pitch had dropped dramatically and started to work on my speech pattern. But the diagnosis was that I had the *formation* of nodules, meaning I had everything set in place for real, full-blown nodules, but no actual nodules. Yet. Nodules are sort of like a corn on your hand. They can be removed, but sometimes just the removal can change the timbre and quality of the voice.

Every once in a while, a doctor wanted to hear a recording of what my voice had sounded like. We played some things from First Gear's albums and some gentle, very well-controlled songs with the Spurrlows. They'd listen, then say, "I'm not sure you're going to get back to that." Well, that was terrifying.

So I had more than nodule formation—I had depression. I had this "why me?" attitude I couldn't shake. I was a young Christian and I thought I was using my voice in the right way for the right reasons. We had reached thousands of kids with the Spurrlows, and held our own in the club scene with First Gear. It was a harsh realization that simply because I was a Christian, doing Christian work, didn't mean everything was going to go right. I could still abuse the tools God gave me.

And this is where Mitzy stepped in. Pregnant, scared about the looming costs of house payments and groceries and our future in general, she marched down to the Board of Education and interviewed to get back into the same school system she'd left two-and-a-half years ago to go on the road with me. She was pretty sure they'd turn her down. Why would they hire a pregnant woman who was due in December, and it's already early-August? They let her get all the way home before they called and offered her a choice of two schools. After a short conference with her mother, she called back and said, "You do know I'm pregnant…" They did, and that was irrelevant to them. She picked a school and stayed there for 28 years.

On top of that, Mitzy has always been extremely frugal and very smart about handling money. I had been making more than the $17-a-week Spurrlow wage, but not a lot more. We had agreed to send home every penny I made on the road. So before Dave Ramsey, before Lonnie was even an idea, before we suspected we would desperately need it, we had an emergency fund.

And then God stepped in. Depressed, anemic, beyond tired from life on the road, unable to sing, I hit a wall. And then I ran. I ran straight to the Bible and into the arms of Jesus. I could've said, "This is bunk. I'm going to go off with my ragged voice and sing rock-and-roll." I could've done something else entirely. In fact, I drove to downtown Louisville and stood in the temp line several times for work. I stood in that line until I was almost at the front to interview, and I just couldn't do it. And it wasn't out of embarrassment. Something inside me was saying, *God has something for you and it isn't in this line. Go back home.*

The only plan I had was to understand what was going on with my voice and why God would allow this to happen. I never blamed God for allowing my vocal problems. I understood then, and continue to believe, all good and perfect gifts come from the Lord. And though it didn't look like it, this was a gift. This was a time of resting and learning. This was a time of being in a room, alone with the Lord, with no one else to lean on, to cling to, no one else speaking for me except Jesus. He was there, listening, saying, *We are going to work through this. We are going to work this out because there's some stuff you'll need for what I've called you and set aside for you to do.*

I started digesting scripture. I read the Psalms. I read the Pauline letters. I read the Old Testament, the New Testament. I had that Bible in my hand all the time. I read and read until one day I got away from the why-me attitude and was able to say, "Lord, if You're going to allow my voice to be taken and my career as a singer, then You must have something awfully good coming. Because You're a good God. The Psalms say it, the letters of Paul say it, the Old Testament says You are a good and perfect God, You have a plan for my life. So if this is part of getting to the plan You have for my life, so be it." And when I was able to say that, it was kind of like a load was lifted. My attitude started changing. I was more hopeful.

After about a year of vocal rest and working with the speech pathologist, the nodule formation went away. I started to practice singing and building up my endurance. I started doing some gigs as a drummer. And then Thurlow Spurr set up an audition in Waco, Texas with pianist and award-winner Kurt Kaiser. My voice still wasn't completely back and, just like Mitzy interviewing pregnant, I thought, *This is gonna be a bust*. My voice is still not where it needs to be to record. But Kurt heard the potential and said, "Let's record this thing." He gave me a few months to work on my voice, then I started to record while occasionally playing drums and singing with choirs in Michigan.

The German philosopher Friedrich Nietzsche famously said, "That which does not kill us makes us stronger." I felt like I was dying on the road with the Gear, and I thought my singing career was dead when I lost my voice. But I learned I'm stronger than that, and God is bigger than all that. One of the songs I took to heart and eventually recorded was "Somebody Bigger Than You and I." That reality sustained me through a difficult time in my life.

I don't remember us ever missing a house payment or having a creditor call or knock on our door. A lot of what I've been able to do musically over the years was because Mitzy had a great job with great benefits, and we relied on God to supply our needs. We learned God loves us and cares for us deeply. We learned God is trustworthy and is the rewarder of all who will diligently seek and pant after Him. We learned God works constantly in our lives—that if we feel He's not with us, we should look around and see how far we've moved because He's always the same. We learned our relationship with Him is solid and real.

We learned a great local church is essential to keeping our eyes on Him and to gaze beyond the things we see with certain faith.

We both come from a long tradition of people who through hard, tough times didn't throw in the towel. My parents were married 50 years and Mitzy's missed 60 years by one month. We've all had arguments and problems and the typical issues every marriage deals with. I'm not saying we handled it better or are better. We've been married more than four decades, and they haven't been perfect. But we share a love of God, our children, our grandchildren, and an attitude of, "We gotta work it out." We're loving our lives together, and we're loving our future together. It will be as the vows go: "Til death do us part." It's been a good run, and we're still on it.

Chapter 5

SINGING FOR THE WORLD

Once I was back in full voice, I regained my confidence. And it showed. In 1975, I began a recording relationship with Word Records and released my first solo album, *Tell It To Jesus*. Noran Spurr was my booking agent from day one, long before my recording career began and, *man*, she was a tough cookie. She was 90 pounds soaking wet and had a delightful combination of quick wit, charming softness and tough negotiator that got me into places I probably would've never attempted myself. Noran always wanted each event to be successful for the sponsors because she knew longevity in the music business meant creating win-win situations for everyone. And people quickly learned she meant what she said.

Noran wasn't afraid to pull out her long-lost and thick West Virginia drawl when she needed to get a chuckle or get your attention.

She honestly believed any serious negotiation went better with a laugh track. Whatever the obstacle in her path, she figured out a way around it with savviness and humor. You can laugh or cry about the things life throws at you. Noran always chose laughter.

But she could go Mama Grizzly Bear on you, too. And I was her cub. I remember one industry function where she overheard something about me she didn't particularly agree with. It was all I could do to get between her and the other person because I knew Noran could render a good tongue-lashing, if she was so motivated. One thing's for certain: I always knew Noran had my back.

Early on, people would often confuse "Larnelle" with "Lionel." That really bothered me because as far back as elementary school, I got called "Lionel" (because of the Lionel trains). As annoying as that was in school, it was even worse being on a platform and getting introduced by another name. So, Noran would patiently spell my name out on the phone, "L-A-R-N-E-L-L-E" over and over again. She had a lot of practice with her own unusual name of Noran Spurr. The misspellings for her name were endless, and one letter came into her office addressed to "Novan Super." That seemed somewhat appropriate. She was a classic original, my biggest fan, and a super woman in many ways.

She died in 2011 after many hard-fought medical issues. One of her favorite songs I recorded was called "His Grace is Greater than my Need," and I was honored to sing it at her home-going.

Knowing Noran, she probably gathered the faithful around while I was singing, pointed downward and said, "See—*that's* how it's done!" Her personal philosophy was simple: strong faith, close family, good friends, and a great sense of humor. She lived every moment of her life that way.

The Gaither Effect

With Noran in charge of booking a relatively unknown solo artist, I started traveling to churches across the U.S. My burgeoning career built slowly with a concert here, an event there. Then, God took my plan of using music to spread the Gospel and exploded it into *bigger* plans the only way He knows how.

Sometime in 1975, Gary McSpadden invited me to sing at his church in Ft. Worth, Texas. Gary was the pastor of First Christian Church and, like most pastors, he was looking for a special event to invite people who were searching for a church community. A concert is a great way to draw people in, as he knew because he was singing baritone in the Gaither Trio then—while still pastoring a church! I didn't know Gary, but we hit it off and developed a special relationship through that concert.

Not long after, the trio came to Louisville and Gary generously invited me backstage in the afternoon to meet everybody. It was exciting and fun, and the concert was a terrific success. That introduction led to an invitation to be part of a Gaither Praise Gathering—an annual event in Indianapolis with up to 14,000 people who came to sing and worship and learn through the ministry of singers and speakers. That led to more opportunities, and it wasn't long before I was invited to join the Gaithers on the road. I sang a couple solos on the tour, but mainly backed up the trio.

And then it got really interesting. In 1980 Bill had spontaneously started a male quartet backstage at a trio concert. Gary sang lead, Bill sang baritone, and two backup singers—Steve Green (formerly a high tenor in Truth) and Lee Young (formerly a bass in Re'generation)—

huddled up with them around the piano and sang "First Day in Heaven." They took it onstage and it was a hit. The New Gaither Vocal Band was born and audiences flocked to hear them. But by 1982, Steve wanted to leave the group to start his own ministry. And that's where I stepped in.

The Vocal Band was pitched to all of us as a group formed by guys who had their own ministries, doing their own things, who wanted to get together and make some great music. And that's what we did. By the time I joined the group, Jon Mohr was singing bass and becoming one of the best storytellers-in-song in the industry. Remember "Find Us Faithful" and "Passin' the Faith Along"? Those came from Jon. Michael English (formerly of The Singing Americans with his signature song, "I Bowed On My Knees [And Cried Holy]") took over the lead when Gary left in 1985.

Some wonderful memories were made on the road with the Gaithers. One of my favorites was when the trio and Vocal Band booked the Fox Theatre in Detroit. The Gaithers had been there many times and always enjoyed a good crowd. As usual, Bill and I wanted to do a little exploring before the concert, find the best place to eat, maybe get some good catfish. So we got off the bus mid-afternoon in downtown Detroit, the streets are teeming with people, most of them black, and Bill—in his propensity to take care of his guys—said, "Larnelle, you probably need to stick pretty close to me as we tool around down here." And I said, "Bill, this is *downtown Detroit*. Look around you—you'd better stay close to *me*!" And he did.

I was with the Vocal Band through 1986. The camaraderie and the brotherhood with those guys was the thing I needed at that time. I loved that I had three brothers probably even more than I enjoyed singing those harmonies. The closeness of these guys—hanging out with them, talking deeply with them, having relationships with them—was critical. I wasn't with them all the time and we didn't share everything in our lives. But standing on that stage with my "brothers" did not mean just singing with them. It was all about the relationships.

That's when music comes alive. That's when the message you're singing about comes alive—when you have a relationship. And those connections are still there. Gary is still a mentor in my life, and I'm so glad he invited to his church in 1975. I could call Jon and talk to him about anything, as well as Bill. Time and distance and life make you move on, but the real test of any meaningful relationship is when you pick up right where you left off no matter how much time apart has passed.

We recorded a reunion DVD in 2008 that reunited all but three of the former and current guys. What fun that was! There I was, sitting amongst all the tenors who'd hit all those incredible high notes, night after night, song after song. It was great to dive back into Suzanne Gaither's funky, up-tempo "Can't Stop Talking About Him," the power ballad, "Dream On," the thoughtfulness of Jon Mohr's "New Point of View." What a journey though song and camaraderie.

Getting It On Tape

Over the years, Bill and Gloria have encouraged so many artists through their ministry. And oftentimes they have said, "Come share with us. We need what you offer at this time in our ministry. And if there is anything you can learn, come learn it. When it comes time for you to go, go with our blessing." In that way, they've taken care of a lot of folks and helped to revive a lot of careers—especially through the Homecoming videos.

Bill had a great love for the sounds of gospel quartets, and he wanted to make sure future generations would be able to hear them long after the artists and groups had passed away. And boy, we needed those sounds on tape. I'm so glad he did that. Those videos came from Bill's desire to gather as many of his childhood southern gospel heroes together onstage as possible, and that experience lead to collections of all kinds of wonderful Christian singers. Singing with all the gang, everybody sitting on stage, the harmonies, being together and having the message through the music jump off that stage and into the hearts of the—those are rich memories.

But the most important part of those concerts and videos were the relationships. I was privileged to be with The Cathedrals one year at Praise Gathering for a satellite concert. The smooth bass singer George Younce and his quartet were southern gospel—and I'm anything but—and they were just so gracious. George picked on his lead, Glen Payne, with his catchphrase, "I love old people!" And they'd launch into "Champion of Love" and I would be clapping right along with the audience. We made our different styles work and the audience seemed to have a great time.

Vestal Goodman was another dear friend I got to know through the Homecoming concerts and DVDs. Vestal had been singing for 40 years by the time I met her and was widely regarded as the Queen of Southern Gospel Music. She knew everybody in the industry, yet she took the time to get to know me. I can still see her waving her trademark handkerchief as she reminded us, "I Wouldn't Take Nothin' For My Journey Now." She called me when my mom passed away with a word of comfort. That's how dear she was. Most of the musical opportunities that came my way were a direct result of developing such wonderful friendships.

But the videos provided another greater value: an opportunity to offer a worship service in people's homes. When Dad was in his later years and his health was failing, we brought him to our home in Louisville. It's said you are once a man and twice a child, and I became Dad's caretaker in his later years. We invited Mitzy's dad, who was also getting on in years, to join us one evening. Neither one of those men felt very good physically on a daily basis. I put a Homecoming tape into the VCR and it wasn't long before the whole house was singing, feet tapping, having a great time. The screen was filled with songs and people Dad and Mr. Sloan and others of their era loved to see and hear, and the songs they sang meant so much to them—so much that, though our dads were failing, they started rejoicing and having church…and forgot about their illnesses a little bit. And that is just one more testimony of how the Gaithers have provided tools of praise the church can use forever.

Joining the Crusade

During those same early years, another exciting thing happened. I was invited to be part of a Billy Graham Crusade. I had heard about Cliff Barrows—cheerful music director and emcee, and George Beverly Shea—big-hearted, bass-baritone gospel singer of "How Great Thou Art," and evangelist Dr. Billy Graham all my life. Of course, my business side knew this was a great career move, but I was soon to learn this was a God-ordained opportunity to be part of something greater than I imagined.

The Sunday morning before the crusade, Mitzy and I attended her family's small church of about 50. The pastor had asked me to sing, so I went to the piano and shared a song in the service. I was nervous and excited and could hardly get through it because I was thinking, *Man… tonight I'm gonna be singing for maybe 50,000…60,000 people! And I'll be identified with probably the most popular crusade team and evangelist of our time!*

I drove to Cincinnati, Ohio that afternoon and arrived at the stadium. I had missed some correspondence about a meeting, and I didn't have a parking pass. Thousands of people are coming to this crusade and I'm driving around, trying to find a place to park! Not a good start. I finally parked and walked up to an usher at the stadium door. I said, "I need to get in, sir. I'm singing here tonight." Well, he looked at me very, very suspiciously. He didn't say anything, just looked at me. I'm thinking he didn't hear me, so I said it again, "I'm singing here tonight. In fact, do you hear that track? That's my song! Surely you've heard it before. My name's Larnelle Harris." Still nothing. There wasn't much I could see going on behind those eyes, except he's looking at somebody who's probably a little delusional. Finally, he looked right into my eyes and out came these words: "Son, are you saved?" At that moment, someone from the production team happened to walk past that door and said, "Larnelle! You gotta come in! Let him in!" So the usher let me in and I sang my song, and it was just part of the fabric of the bigger things going on that night.

I learned a couple of lessons that day: (1) singing for 50 people in Sunday morning church is just as important as singing for 50,000 in a stadium, and (2) being part of the crusade team was not just a career opportunity to build our own names. It was a chance to build the name of Christ.

Dr. Graham preached a wonderful sermon that night, as he always does. And then in that characteristic way we've all seen on TV and in person, he presented a very simple message of love and grace, gave the invitation, then stood back out of the way. And that was my third lesson: Just do what God has called you to do, then move back and watch God work. The entire crusade team on the stage that night physically and emotionally took a step back, folded our arms, and were privileged to watch people coming forward from all areas of that stadium—from the highest seats, from the floor, from every place, they were coming. They were coming, not because I sang and not even because of Dr. Graham's sermon, but because the Spirit of God was moving in that place.

The question the usher asked me when I was trying to get into the stadium became the most important question of the evening. God was there, asking us to assess our relationships with Him with that same, simple question: "Are you saved?" Thousands of people answered that question that night and started on the road to a great relationship with Christ. And many of us who knew the Lord already were taken to another plateau in our Christian walks.

I was privileged to be a guest on the crusades and other Graham events for about 30 years, and my experience was just fabulous. The whole team—whether permanent members or guests—was very gracious and welcoming. Tedd Smith was a wonderful pianist and generous man, and John Innes kept up with him, note for note, on the organ. The choir burned every word of "Just As I Am, Without One Plea" into our hearts. I will never forget sitting on the platform and watching the effect of Bev singing, "I'd Rather Have Jesus." Evie Tornquist took the stage with "Born Again" and charmed everyone with her sweet spirit. Steve Green blew the roof off with "A Mighty Fortress," and Sandi Patty joined me to sing "More Than Wonderful" during a 1984 televised crusade. None of that would have been possible without Grady Wilson, tour manager, traveling aide, bodyguard and backstage comedian. Such great memories. Such a great team.

Every time I was invited to be with the crusade team seemed monumental to me. Hearing the simple, unadulterated gospel and invitation, watching Dr. Graham fold his arms and wait, taking himself out of the way as we watched thousands of people come to the altar to give their lives to Christ…there's nothing more monumental than being part of that.

Becoming a Promise Keeper

In 1994, I accepted an invitation to be a guest singer for a new concept started by Bill McCartney, former head football coach at the University of Colorado. He had this idea to gather men together in a place where both he and they would be comfortable: sports arenas. Then he would challenge them through speakers and music and group discussions to celebrate their Biblical manhood and motivate them toward Christ-like masculinity. He gave them seven promises to make to become men of integrity. Then he sent them home as Promise Keepers.

It was a novel concept and few people were sure it would even work. But let me tell you: It worked! And maybe no one was more surprised than me. I didn't think you could get 50,000 men to anything I knew about except sports. Yet, I stood on the stage in Folsom Field—a giant, open-air, horseshoe-shaped stadium with the Rocky Mountains in the background—filled to the brim with 52,000 men singing "How Great Thou Art"…singing every word of "To God Be the Glory." I had never heard 50,000 men sing hymns. The only word to describe it is *amazing*.

I was a featured guest at many Promise Keepers conferences across the U.S.—at the Indianapolis Hoosier Dome where people could hear 62,000 men singing "Amazing Grace" from two blocks away, at Columbia's Williams-Brice Stadium where 83,000 men stood up and sang, "Stand Up For Jesus," at Pittsburgh's Three Rivers Stadium where passersby found 44,000 men singing "In Christ Alone" haunting and beautiful, at Chicago's Soldier Field where the choir, dressed in black T-shirts with the slogan "Real Men Sing Real Loud" led 73,000 manly voices in "A Mighty Fortress Is Our God." The atmosphere was always electric. Combine the chanting and high-fiving of Monday Night Football with a 12-piece band and gospel choir, and the emotion of those old-time revivals in the giant tabernacles, and you have the picture. *Amazing*.

But maybe the best thing Coach Mac and his crew did was create a pot of boiling water where real life issues rose to the top. Generational families came to these events—grandfathers, sons, grandsons—and they all had issues they needed to deal with. One of those issues was racism, and that's why the leaders of Promise Keepers brought me on board.

One of the "Seven Promises of Promise Keepers" is: "A Promise Keeper is committed to reaching beyond any racial and denominational barriers to demonstrate the power of biblical unity." A lot of the older guys in attendance had fled to the suburbs during the inner-city racial tensions of the 1950s and 60s. They'd never dealt with their feelings on race, their attitudes about integration, their thoughts about equality. But I had...and still was. I had struggled with them as a kid in the backwoods of Kentucky, as a traveling member of the Spurrlows, and as a father raising black children. I had a lot of thoughts about racial tension, and Coach Mac thought Steve Green and I could work those into an original song for a mixed audience with a racial disconnect.

Out of all that came "Teach Me To Love." In the song, you hear me trying to help someone understand the plight of black America—"All my life I've had to struggle to be free"…then you hear Steve singing an apology for having prejudice—"Show me all the pride and arrogance that tear our souls apart…" Our intent was not to cause anger or guilt, but to open the door for discussions with these men.

Coach Mac also brought in Dr. Tony Evans to speak about racism. Tony is a pastor, author and broadcaster who also served as chaplain for the Dallas Mavericks and Cowboys. He knows sports and he knows men. He'd take the stage and say, "The Bible doesn't talk about black Christians or white Christians—there isn't any such thing. The Bible doesn't separate us. You become a Christian, you belong to Jesus." And that was the bottom line to the issue.

He would lay it all out for them, then Steve and I would sing "Teach Me To Love," and the response was incredible. Scores of men came down to the stadium fields, knelt, and handed over their racial baggage to the Lord. These were the same guys who'd just sung "Amazing Grace." I remember walking amongst them, praying with them as they cried and hugged and did their best to deal with an issue they should have dealt with a long time ago. Those moments touched my heart and helped me deal with my own residual issues.

Those were "mountaintop" moments. Everything's good when you're on the mountain—you're feeling good, you have been challenged by a talented, Biblical speaker, you have heard the Word, you have learned how insidious sin is and how it will ruin your physical and spiritual health. You have laid it all out and left it at the cross. It's an incredible thing, and it was great to play a small role in those powerful moments.

Seeing the World – Russia

In 1991, Jim Groen of the Worldwide Leadership Council invited me to be part of The Moscow Project—an ecumenical push to get four million New Testament Bibles into Russian hands. I joined about 250 musicians and missionaries from all over the world for a weeklong blitz of concerts in Russia that would end with a rally, gospel music festival, and Bible giveaway inside the Kremlin.

This was a very big deal at that time. We were on high alert because the coup to save the Communist Party started and failed that year. We watched the news coverage in the States, saw the people and tanks in the street. In fact, the coup was still happening as we prepared to travel there and we had many discussions about whether we should go or not. We were walking into a risky, possibly even life-threatening situation, so the organizers told us, "This is dangerous…do you want to come?" We did, and I'm so glad we went.

Not quite a year earlier, President Boris Yeltsin and his Soviet government had followed through on a promise of religious freedom by passing a ground-breaking law. Jim Groen wanted to jump right in and capitalize on this law. Jim has always been involved in ministries that go into a country and teach the gospel to lay people, instill a solid knowledge of the foundational principles of the Bible, then send them out to witness to their friends, neighbors, relatives, acquaintances. We went to Russian with those lay people—Russian Christians who know the language and customs, who know what to say, what not to say, who have examples and stories relatable to people who live there.

We arrived and hopped on a train to St. Petersburg. In the middle of the night, the train was stopped by Russian troops. We were all sleeping and had to get up and stand by while the troops searched the train, searched the passengers. One soldier opened a box in my stateroom and found some cassettes—all with my picture on them. Contraband. I remember the soldier looking through them and saying, "Why so many tapes?" I simply handed him one. He took it, looked at me, and that was the end of it. The experience was a little tense—that kind of thing doesn't happen in the U.S.—but I didn't feel like we were in serious danger.

We performed concerts in cities with tanks parked in the street. In 1991, there was a real premium on food, so we saw people standing in many lines to get the basic staples, much like in the pictures of the Great Depression. You know what else they were standing in line for? Bibles.

Americans can't really understand what it's like to have a Bible shortage—to worship in "underground" churches, sharing sections you've carefully torn from the original so everybody could have some scripture to take home and study. For the most part, we have no concept of facing discrimination, being denied access to higher education, getting passed over for the best jobs...because of our faith. Some of the bible distributions were like mob scenes—men, women, children grabbing for Bibles. They were desperate for the Word.

At the end of our concert and distribution tour, we set up our sound and lights inside the Kremlin's walls in the main hall of the Palace of Congresses. Even before we landed in the country, Jim was there and walked around the Kremlin, much like Joshua before the battle of Jericho. We were all praying for God to move in a powerful way. The 6,000-seat concert hall was filled to capacity. We sang, the Rev. Billy Kim preached a fiery sermon and half of the attendees stood up and accepted Christ.

Nothing in American life could have prepared me for that scene— hungry people reaching out for the gospel in any form they could get... written, spoken, sung. As so many times before and since, I was chosen to be part of an event that would bless other people, but it ended up blessing me more.

Seeing the World – South Africa

In 1993, I stepped back into national controversy with a series of concerts in South Africa. Although this fractured country was gearing up for an historic democratic election, the concert promoters—Lindsay and Michele Dillman—wanted desperately to bring Christian music to their country. What better time than this—tribal leaders fighting for control, ethnic youth calling for all-out war against the government and whites in general, politics driving a slaughterhouse mentality—to sing a message of God's love and grace?

Mitzy and our daughter Teresa accompanied me, and we had endured multiple inoculations, health department warnings not to drink the water, to take packaged snacks and mouthwash to brush our teeth to avoid dysentery. We had been so prepped and warned and sternly cautioned that when we stepped off our 15-hour flight, we were sure we would encounter our first lion in the open. Instead, we saw the sprawling and modern metropolis of Johannesburg. It was absolutely stunning. At the evening concerts, I told the crowds we had to be inoculated to travel there and they would just crack up!

We stopped in Pretoria—one of three capital cities—in the northern part of Gauteng Province. The locals call it "Jacaranda City" because of the thousands of purple-blue Jacaranda trees blooming along the streets. Just stunning. We gaped at the flat-topped Table Mountain overlooking Cape Town. We were treated to an authentic Afrikaans meal that looked a lot like chitlins. Everywhere we went, the land was lush and fragrant and bursting with local pride.

But an undercurrent of unrest was woven into everything. This proud and beautiful nation was desperately trying to break free from 46 years of "apartheid"—enforced segregation into "black," white," "coloured," and "Indian"—where education, medical care, social and civil rights, everything really, was separated. The country stood on the edge of a racial firestorm. I was on a television show—"Good Morning, South Africa"—on the anniversary of the 1976 Soweto Uprising, where close to 700 black students were gunned down by police at a rally-turned-riot for better (more equal) education. Our guides refused to take us there, citing dangerous times. Nobody went to work that day.

One of our biggest concerts was in Durban, the busiest port in South Africa and a tourist hub with its Golden Mile of Indian Ocean beachfront. It's a metropolitan area, but we were there just before Nelson Mandela (newly freed from 27 years in prison) and Mangosuthu Buthelezi (founder of the Inkatha Freedom Party) were set to address a crush of South Africans at a rugby stadium just across the street from our concert venue. Teresa told me someone was following her there, and we discovered we had a security detail because of the social climate.

The streets were packed with a mix of people in tribal dress and cosmopolitan suits, tribal "diviners" wearing colorful beads and goat bladders in their hair, leopard skins and ox-hide shields—much like we would see at a multi-cultural pop festival. Emotions were high. The people loved their country and wanted to fix it. The balcony inside our venue actually shook during the concert. They seemed to welcome our message of God's love and we loved being there with them.

It's still a struggling democracy. I've sung in grand auditoriums and lush churches, small halls in remote townships, and in the middle of nowhere among tribes of people suffering from AIDS who still danced and shouted and rejoiced in the Lord. In one isolated village in Malawi, I was dumbfounded by the incredible distance villagers had to walk to get drinkable water. I could not comprehend that kind of hardship. Shortly after that visit, Feed the Children—a nonprofit relief organization—let me be part of building a well for that village. The villagers sent me a photo of them standing around that well, and it means more to me than any Dove or Grammy award given me. Because long after I'm gone, and no one remembers the name Larnelle Harris, that same well will be there in that village, providing hope and life to people.

Seeing the World – South Korea

In 1973, Dr. Billy Kim translated for Graham's five-day Seoul, Korea Crusade. More than 1.1 million people sat on the People's Plaza—

formerly the famous "Quay 16" landing ground of the Korean War—and heard Dr. Graham's message through the enthusiasm of Dr. Kim. More than 12,000 rose to their feet the last night when Dr. Graham challenged them with, "If you're willing to forsake all other gods, stand up." He led them in the prayer of accepting Christ, and the church began fantastic growth in South Korea.

In 2004, 30 years later, Dr. Kim invited me to join him to continue spreading the Gospel in South Korea, including Suwon Central Baptist Church in Seoul—his church that started with ten members in 1960 and had grown to 7,000 by the time I visited. He was president of Baptist World Alliance, very influential, and speaking around the world, but he still had time for me. That's the kind of man he is. He retired shortly after I visited.

I worshiped with a crowd of 50,000 on Yoi Island one Wednesday night in Dr. David Cho's Yoido Full Gospel Church—part of the largest Pentecostal Christian congregation (830,000) in South Korea. I visited several Korean churches that tour, thanks to the sponsorship of Dr. Kim's media group.

Although these churches are very large, there's a tenderness to the gospel they proclaim…maybe because in that part of the world it's not all that popular to be a Christian. They appreciated the music, that we took the time to visit, that we would struggle through their language and speak a phrase or two. They stood and worshipped and applauded. It was a good time.

On a return trip to South Korea, I visited U.S. troops stationed at the 38th Parallel between North and South Korea. I was given a 1-Star General Classification and landed on the base in one of those infamous Blackhawk helicopters with the same surprise I've felt every time I visit. You'd think the dividing line between two countries that are so close and have been at war for 60 years with totally different political ideologies would be louder. You'd think there'd be more hustling and bustling in

this area, with military trucks running hither and yon, with men and women screaming at each other, trying to shout each other's beliefs down.

But it's a very quiet place. A very somber place. I've stood in the building where disputes are handled. There is an invisible—but very real—line down the middle of that building, even down the middle of the negotiating table. Outside are guards staring at each other over that line. If one of them moves wrong or even flinches, chaos could ensue... war could erupt.

So you can imagine the concern flowing through the U.S. families stationed there on their second or third tours. The Armed Forces duplicated our *American Spirit* CD and gave about 8,000 of them to soldiers returning to active, frontline duty. Six songs were on there— "Let Freedom Ring," "Beginning With You," "Statue of Liberty," "Mighty Spirit," "The Star-Spangled Banner," and the title track I wrote after the attack of 9/11. Every once in a while, I hear from or run into someone who says, "I was in Afghanistan (or Iraq), and I heard your song and, boy, it was like a piece of home." That brings me such joy and peace.

I've been to other places like the 38th Parallel—Checkpoint Charlie at the Berlin Wall, the Green Line between Israel and its neighbors, the Kremlin. I don't understand all the reasons for such places as these. But my prayer is that one day, through God's intervention and grace, the world's need for them will vanish.

Seeing the World – Israel

Two of my favorite Gaither recording experiences happened in Israel in 2005. The first time I went, I was being interviewed and the reporter asked, "What is it like to be in Israel?" And I said without thinking, "It's like being home." And the interviewer just froze, as though she couldn't think of any comment. Upon reflection, she probably felt the same.

I sang, "Amen" for *Israel Homecoming*, and "I Walked Today Where Jesus Walked" for *Jerusalem Homecoming*. And I have walked where Jesus walked—the streets are all there, all those Old Testament places and names of the lineage and genealogy. I have been to Israel a number times and walked down the Via Dolorosa. I have had devotions on the Sea of Galilee, I have stood on the Masada where Herod built his palaces, and I have been to the tomb where Jesus was laid. By the way, He's not there. I have walked those streets and stood in those places, and I have been overwhelmed with the feeling I was somewhere I was supposed to be.

That same year, Discovery House asked me to host a televised broadcast of their two-part exclusive, *Pressing On: A Musical Special on the Life of the Apostle Paul.* While filming in the citadel of David about Paul's struggles to shape the early church, we noticed a summer camp with Palestinian and Jewish children playing together by design. I thought how important it was to help these children grow up, learning something about each other besides hate. There is such palpable tension in Israel—at the airport, near the West Bank, in Jerusalem…tension that dates back to the time of Ishmael and Isaac. It's an age-old skirmish that makes me wonder if the struggle will ever resolve.

And yet… The people will listen very openly to songs about Jesus. They're always willing to discuss and entertain various viewpoints. I was told a story about a bunch of Baptist preachers who wanted to convert the Israeli tour guide showing them around. The preachers said, "We're right here at the Red Sea. We can baptize you, brother, and make you complete—make you a Messianic Jew!" And our guide responded with: "I will let you baptize me, if you will let me circumcise you." Everybody had a big laugh and that was the end of the witnessing attempt.

I've found if I just sing the message of Christ, it does what it does. God will honor my willingness to be involved in what He's doing around the world. I sang for a wine-tasting event there once. I said, "I'm not here to convince you of anything. I am going to sing these songs and worship my Lord." And at the end, the guy who introduced me said, "You know what? If that's Christianity, I may take a look at it."

The message gets the same reception here in the States. In 2013, I joined pianist Dino Kartsonakis, Sandi Patty, visionary leader/bridge-builder Robert Stearns, choirs and orchestras for the "Honoring Israel at Carnegie Hall" event. A number of U.S. government dignitaries were seated there with Israeli diplomats, Jews and Messianic Jews. And again, I was surprised at how they responded to songs about Jesus. When I sang, "I Walked Today Where Jesus Walked," they applauded, even stood to their feet and cheered. When Sandi and I sang, "I've just seen Jesus…I know that He's alive…" they did the same thing. If they were responding to the performance, that's OK—we're still getting the Word in.

Everywhere I've traveled, I've encountered people who are hungry, thirsty for God's love. I feel so fortunate God provides just the right place at just the right time—His place, His time—to share His message. Even if *one person* hears and receives the Gospel of Jesus, the trip was worth it.

Chapter 6

THE CREATIVE PROCESS

When it came time to record as a solo artist, I searched long and hard for what I wanted to say, and I wasn't always sure what it should be. I knew I loved the Lord, and I wanted to sing about Him, but I was continually learning who I was as a person and as a performer. I didn't want to make any mistakes. So, I had to put myself in a place where I could go beyond singing and performing music, and move into learning the intricacies of *writing* music, then the process of recording.

I found out very early, if you don't have an idea of who you are—especially as a young artist—somebody will tell you. People are standing in the wings, ready to insist you should record *this* kind of music. You should sound *that* way. You should change it up. And they may or may not be right.

So I dove into the writing and recording processes with my college background of French chanson, German lieder, and Elizabethan love songs, my childhood love of James Brown and Jimmy McGriff and all things jazz, and my serious study of voice and percussion. And I surrounded myself with people who really knew what they were doing. Here's what I learned along the way.

Finding 10

When we're ready to put together a new CD, "10" is the magic number. What I discovered is it's quite a task to find 10 great songs—not songs with a great rhythm but shaky lyrics, or killer lyrics but predictable music. *Great* songs. It's a tall order requiring talent and effort and patience.

So, we put out feelers nationwide to find out who's writing what. For me, it comes down to finding a big, universal idea—something that appeals to most people, a story people can hear in a song that relates to part of their own life stories. It's always a good place to start, because it really makes me think through what I want to say and how I want to say it. Then once the idea clicks, the real work begins.

The Words

Lyric writing is a fascinating process. I have written some songs by myself and in a collaborative effort with other writers. In the end, I want the best lyrics I can find.

Sometimes an idea sparks and the lyrics are written in a short time. But most of the time songwriting is simply hard work, searching for just the right word or phrase. I like to think there are songs that are written or crafted well, and songs that are "made up." For me, there's a big difference. A made-up song may rhyme and have some of the right phrases in it, but it might also have trite lines or tired sayings that won't challenge the listener. The theme might wander. Those are big pitfalls and become easy to recognize.

Early in my songwriting career, I carried around an idea book so I could write lyrics in my spare time and while traveling. I would change one line of a lyric and then another line wouldn't work. I would write a chorus and it wouldn't fit with the verse. Then I would find a line in the verse that was weak. It's a process requiring a lot of patience, time and thought. And it made me appreciate great writers who continually put in the effort to find ideas and phrases that are both universal and challenging to the listener.

I think it's also essential not to sing in "code." Christianity has buzzwords Christians understand—like "saved" and "redeemed" and "rapture"—but nonbelievers or even new believers don't fully grasp. Those words are very real and important, but can be confusing to people who haven't read much of the Bible or been in good churches where they hear those concepts explained. To keep the idea universal and understandable, we have to speak and sing in plain English. A lot of today's great writers understand you can't require the listener to get a Biblical dictionary to look up buzzwords.

Every once in a while, we have a lyric some think is just too direct. There was a time when "Jesus" was not really alright to say, believe it or not. More than one time, in order to make a song universal, someone suggested I use the word "you" instead of "Jesus." I've refused to do that most of the time—although "I Miss My Time With You" doesn't have the name of Jesus in it at all, but that was a unique song spoken from God's point of view. At other times, I consider the suggestion because it makes the lyric clearer and more poetic.

I have also been approached with songs that were very good, but were not crafted right or the concept was not biblically sound. There have been times when people insisted, "This is going be a big song. People are going to listen to this…they're going to hear this." But it wasn't sound to me. Something was "off" or even wrong in a verse and I've had to say, "I'm sorry. I don't care how big that song is going to be.

It's not resonating with me. Maybe another artist can say it, but I can't." They may keep insisting it's gold, and I've had to say—as have other artists and friends—"Well, that may be. Radio may play it and it may be all over TV. I hope it does well. But I'm not going to record that." I've always felt if I recorded something I didn't really believe in or wasn't true to the gospel, I would lose the trust of people who give me 40 minutes of their time, listening to me sing on a recording.

Sometimes the lyric is fine, but it just doesn't hit me right because of my own growth and experience with the Lord. That's been the lyrical key for me over the years: If I can't take a swab and do a Biblical forensic test on it and find it somewhere in my Christian DNA, then I can't record it. I won't record it. It might be a good song, but there's nothing in me that can say that. I think all artists need to keep that in mind because when a song does become a hit, they will be singing it for a long, long time.

And sometimes the lyric is older or younger than me. Starting out, I was pitched some songs that were experiential, and I had not lived those lyrics yet. I had no basis for making the words real when I would sing it. So I couldn't sing it. Later, some lyrics talked about experiences I had years ago, but I had moved on from them. It's all about the responsibility of Christian growth. I'm older and more experienced. I understand the song's concept, but it needs to be sung by someone younger. Sometimes we found a very, very good song—written

correctly, crafted well—that really didn't say what God had on my heart at that time to be saying. So then a very good song became a song I couldn't use.

It's a Production

I've always enjoyed talking to Don Butler, longtime president of the Gospel Music Association, about the industry and what makes a great song. He has a phrase I've always remembered: "Right song, right artist." The perfect song needs the right music paired with the right lyric to make an idea blossom and live within the heart. Then the right artist needs to sing it.

Some great lyricists and singers are very good at writing the music, too. Scott Krippayne released 10 very well-received albums of his own, but he may be even better known for what he did for other Christian singers, like Point of Grace, Sandi Patty, John Tesh, and me. "But God," "Soon," and "If Not for the Storm" all became the songs they are because of Scott's contributions. Songwriters Steve Siler and Tony Wood were indelible parts of those hits, too. Dave Clark has written more than 40 Christmas and Easter musicals, and was integral to five of my #1 songs.

Once the lyric/music package is together, we give it to an arranger/ programmer and producer to do their thing. Now the song goes through another set of scrutinizing eyes. Sometimes we'll be in the studio, recording a song, and a line just doesn't hit me right—it just doesn't feel right. And maybe it's the difference in the way the music is arranged—a stress, a beat, a cadence—and the marriage of the lyric and music can feel totally out of place. This has happened many times, and that's when we often rewrite a portion of the song during the recording process.

When preparing to record *The Father Hath Provided* album, the orchestra was booked and producer Greg Nelson suddenly gave Dave

Clark and me a task of coming up with a lyric to some music by Dove Award winner Don Koch. The orchestra would be there in the morning to record the music, and we had to have the lyrics by session time! That created some angst, but also excitement because we had to come through with the right concept and words on a tight deadline. And we did. That song became the title cut.

Sometimes as we're in the studio listening to a song, someone has an idea like cutting a verse. "We need to get back to the chorus as fast as possible, because that's the hook," they might say. Those kinds of cuts can make a song more appealing. But it's a gamble. Sometimes you just don't know what will happen. In one case, I was asked to cut the second verse for this very reason. Well, sometimes if you cut a verse, you haven't told the whole story. A big part becomes missing. So I flat-out refused to do that. It was tense, but I won that battle, we recorded it and the song, "I Miss My Time With You," went to #1 on the charts. In that particular instance, my instincts were right.

Finally, we mix all the elements together and I begin performing it in concert to see how people respond. Most of the time, it's a great response. Sometimes a church or Christian organization doesn't want me to sing about "the blood" or "rapture" or certain Christian principles. They want me to cut certain things—not because they aren't understandable, but because they just don't talk about "that." In most cases, I respectfully decline to make those cuts. The song is complete once it reaches the performance stage, and I believe it has received God's blessing.

And that's the process we've used over the years in recording songs. My intention is to either write or find a great lyric wrapped in great music in the genre that delivers it best, then sing it with everything in my heart. I hope those people under the sphere of my influence found I've done that.

Finding a Calling

One of the questions I get asked a lot, I usually don't answer directly. But I'm going to answer it now. People often ask: "Should I pursue singing or songwriting as a career?"

I had the same question in mind when I first started. I remember playing the drums with Roy Clark and the Las Vegas orchestra one time during my Sparrow years. It was a challenge but a lot of fun and in fact, I made friends with a few of the players who were in the musicians union there. One afternoon, they invited me to the union hall for what I thought would be a jam session. One of the arrangers brought in a Johnny Carson-esque composition with that big band sound. He passed out the music, counted off and the guys and gals jumped right in playing that arrangement as it they had played it a hundred times before. Because I played drums, I kept a close eye on the drummer. Now I was a good drummer, but this guy was a *great* drummer. I left the hall that day wondering if I could ever play like that.

I had the same epiphany with sports. Some years back, I got a package from Bunny Davis, a Danville sports hero. His nickname "Bunny" says it all. He was legendary in Danville and other parts of Kentucky, and maybe even the country, because of his speed and agility on the field. He included some newspaper clippings he had come across from my days of basketball in high school. I was a pretty good player in my teens, and I remember being torn between pursuing sports or music when I enrolled at Western Kentucky University. That is, until I played in a pickup game with some of the scholarship players who were more than serious about basketball. WKU was the starting place for several well-know players and coaches, such as Clem Haskins and Jim McDaniels and Greg Smith, just to name a few, who played professionally. During that game I realized something. The game they were playing I knew not of.

Moments like those helped me decide the direction of my life. I was beginning to understand that eagerness often times mimics inspiration.

One thing I noticed in myself and in some others, is how eager we are to be on the big stage. However, when God commanded Moses to tell Pharaoh to let the Israelites go, Moses began making excuses as he checked his background for the man-acquired knowledge to complete the task to which God was calling him. There was a reluctance. I felt an enormous sense of responsibility and reluctance about handling the nuggets of God — His holy scripture — His word through music.

Moses figured out that is was God doing the calling when he saw God use his staff to do the miraculous. I have always felt that I was called to serve God through music. And have been continually challenged to understand ministry is about God.

Dave Clark and I wrote a song built around that scriptural truth. The song is entitled "Greater Still." John the Baptist said it this way, "I must become less that He (Jesus) become greater still. To this day, I find myself going through a check of personal motives regardless of the event or opportunity, a practice that should be embraced by every Christian.

Once afternoon, a neighbor brought some of the songs he had written that he used in outings with the children of his church. I never want to tell anybody what they should or shouldn't do regarding their art, but I said, "You need to keep singing these. These songs are important to those kids." Will a major artist record any of his songs? Maybe not. Probably not. But they had a purpose. God was using them as He will use anyone who submits their lives and talents to Him.

So, should you sing or write? Bear in mind you might be on this earth to sing at a kids' camp or the local jail. I accompanied my pastor to a nursing home recently and sang a couple of songs for the residents. One older gent came up to me and said, "You know, you might think about singing for a living!" Just because you don't sing for thousands or write songs that the masses will hear doesn't mean that you aren't being used by God.

In 1 Chronicles 15:22, King David is appointing musicians for the celebrations and festivals. He chose to put in charge of the singers a man named Chenaniah, leader of the Levites. And why? Because He was skilled. One translation even says, "Because he was very good at it." So, I'll answer the question by asking one that should seem obvious by now. Are you really good at singing or songwriting? If so, God can use you in the music ministry. If the honest answer is that you are not, then know that God has many areas of His Kingdom-building where you can be used.

I've been given many awards and accolades over the years. But I heard a pastor say at a memorial service words that I have never forgotten. "No awards are needed to hear God say at the end of life's journey, 'Well done thou good and faithful servant.'" The ultimate goal, whatever area of ministry you are in, is to announce, announce, proclaim, proclaim the mighty works of our God.

Chapter 7

THE SONGS

E very successful musician eventually has a chance to walk back through history and find a performance or song that created a career-defining moment. Here are some of mine.

"More Than Wonderful"

Producer Don Marsh called me one day in 1984 and asked if I would like to do a song with a young lady by the name of Sandi Patty. Well, I had heard of Sandi, of course. Everybody had heard of her! And I said, "You know, let me pray about that for a little bit. Hang on for just a second... Dear Lord, YES!" I said. "Man, that would be great!"

Lanny Wolf had written a power anthem for the Christmas musical *Thou Shall Call His Name Jesus*. The producers were saying, "We've got something here. It's working as a solo, but it needs something else. It needs two voices that can breathe life into it." Now, Sandi wasn't on the solo recording, but Don thought blending our voices together might just work.

Because of our schedules, Sandi and I couldn't get together to record it in the studio. So they brought in another soprano and we started listening and working out the parts, and decided this just might work. So I recorded my part and Sandi recorded hers a few days later.

About six months later, I was getting off a plane from St. Louis, waiting at baggage claim and a stranger walks up to me, touches me on the shoulder and with tears in her eyes, says, "I love that duet." And I said, "What duet?" By that time, the song was playing everywhere…and I didn't even know it.

My recollection is it wasn't until an early-80s Gaither Praise Gathering conference in Indianapolis that someone suggested we sing the duet live. I basically knew my part, but we had never performed it together. So we went upstairs to a little room with a cassette player and rehearsed. Then we stepped out on the stage in front of what must have been 10,000 people, and we started to sing. By the middle of it, people were already on their feet, praising the Lord. I barely remember getting through it. I was so wrapped up in what the song said and what it was doing that when it was over, it was like silence in my ears. People were standing and clapping, but I didn't hear them. It was such a worshipful experience. I remember being so thankful God had chosen me to be part of introducing this wonderful idea to the world.

The lyric, drawn from Ephesians 3, says, "Now to Him who is able to do exceedingly abundantly above all that we ask or think…" So He's *more* than wonderful…God is always giving us more, and asking us for more. The song provokes us to ask ourselves: Who or what is God to you? What does the love of God mean *to* you and *for* you? What has it meant to you since giving yourself to Him, since your conversion? God's love is more than anything I could ever think or ask about. And people are still responding to that message because it helps them explain their testimony. "He's more than wonderful, more than miraculous." He is all that and more.

A lot of things came together at that point. Everybody knew this was about to be a big song. Then Sandi recorded a live LP at an Assembly of God church in Lakeland, Florida. I came in as kind of a surprise, and the same thing happened—people worshipped as they heard these two musicians share this lyric and this song. It put us together as a duo, and we've been singing it together ever since.

Singing with Sandi over the years has created special moments for both of us. I'm so glad the relationship surrounding the song has taken on a significance that's bigger than any of the parts. I go to places and people say, "Did you bring Sandi?" And she goes somewhere and hears, "Did you bring Larnelle?" To be totally honest, a solo artist doesn't necessarily want to hear that. But you know what? It's a good thing. I feel so thankful and fortunate to be used to bring that message into the world—one the whole world has heard.

We recorded this song again, 30 years later, on a floating studio—the *ms Nieuw Amsterdam* from the Holland Cruise Line—during the Sandi & Friends cruise. Nobody was in the room but us and the engineers. What an experience! I was so thankful that 30 years later we could pull it off. And we didn't just pull it off! I believe God allowed us to practice all those years and all those times so it could be a new thing for us and for the audience. And the song still has it—it still says the same thing, and gets the same reaction. It helps people look back on their relationships and grasp what being in the arms of the Lord means to them.

I understood at the beginning this was a great song. When Don Marsh called, I knew right away it was going to be what it became. From a professional standpoint, I knew doing a song with Sandi would be a wonderful career move. I understood a lot of people would hear it. I also understood there were people who would hear it and be moved and blessed by it and want to hear it again. But after living with it some 30 years, it's become so much more to me than a great career move. It's not just two people singing together. Because today I know this: God is more wonderful to me now in my 60s than he was in my 20s.

I'm so thankful God used Sandi and I to be part of introducing an idea surrounded by music that would help people express their testimonies. When you think you have exhausted everything He is, you're just scratching the surface.

It's a different song to me now. "Well, I tried Him and I found His promises are true…" lyrics like that are bigger than the sum of their parts.

"I've Just Seen Jesus"

Sandi and I were in Israel in 1985 during an event with Bill Gaither, and had spent some time talking about the possibility of doing another duet and putting it on my album. From a radio play and concert performance point of view, reactions to "More Than Wonderful" were positive. I was getting ready to record my seventh album, so producer Greg Nelson and I went out actively looking for other duet possibilities. Thankfully, everyone was submitting songs to us, and many of them would have made great duets. But we were looking for a special song.

Then, in walked Bill Gaither with an idea he and Gloria had been working on for a long time. He played it for us in the studio and the song was entitled, "I've Just Seen Jesus." Special songs come along just every once in a while. And boy, when they do, they do something to the hairs on your arm. Those words raised the hairs on all of our arms in the studio. We were overjoyed because it seemed this was what we were looking for. It was a big, universal idea that put to rest all the naysayers who say God is dead or nonexistent. "I've just seen Jesus," says the chorus. "I tell you, He's alive."

Bill and a new, young songwriter named Danny Daniels wrote the music. At the time, Bill had an old portable Silvertone cassette recorder/player he used for recording melodies. He and Danny did a four-hands, one-piano rendition of "I've Just Seen Jesus" with Danny playing the accompaniment and Bill banging out the melody. Bill brought that tape to the studio and David Clydesdale used that rendition of bass movements and chord progressions almost verbatim to arrange and orchestrate the song. David really knows how to surround a lyric with woodwinds and brass and percussion to make it live. And by the way—that was Danny Daniels' first attempt at songwriting!

Gloria Gaither wrote the lyric, but the second verse needed a rework—it was a really long, big production kind of thing, and we just needed three minutes' worth. Bill got on the phone with Gloria because we liked everything but that second verse, and she reworked it and made it a great, great story.

Bill and Gloria are known for finding those big ideas wherever they come from—intellectually or dropped out of Heaven, or a combination of both. Sandi and I went in purposely this time and recorded it separately, again. We knew exactly what we were doing the second time around—or, more accurately, the people involved—the Gaithers, Danny, David, Greg—knew what we would do.

We didn't just stand there and start singing parts. We were coached into it with musical nuance. They knew, when we do this, Larnelle and Sandi are going to do that. When this modulation or chord cadence comes up, Sandi will do this, Larnelle will do that. Bill and Danny knew what the arrangers would do, Greg knew with certain touches what David would do, and David knew how to color the music in such a way that we would hear the hints and make the right choices. It might have been even better that we weren't together in the studio, so all of these little plays could take place. After the song was finished, Bill called Danny and said, "We've got a hit." It premiered at Praise Gathering in the fall of 1985 and it was, indeed, a hit.

Musically, it's a sneak-attack kind of song. It begins with an easy, mysterious vibe, then starts to build until it's a freight train at the end. That was intentional on Bill and Danny's part. They wrote a minor-major movement in harmonic progression that's just perfect for the lyric. The verse is dramatic and dark and in a minor key, which makes the major key of the chorus really stand out. And then it works up into high drama.

I think people like seeing that drama—two people dramatically challenging each other. Sandi and I have both been through a lot of stuff, and when we look into each other's eyes and sing that lyric, now it's not just a song anymore. "All that I'd done before won't matter anymore." That's a huge statement. Jesus is the ultimate forgiver. There's always a second chance…He never throws us away.

I have sung it with some other sopranos who were worried about the high notes, and I said, "You know what, just tell the story. You don't have to do anything." Nothing makes this song—the song makes itself. "All that I'd done before" doesn't matter because He's alive! That is a message hounding the world since the days of the Old Testament.

In fact, people were hearing the song and every time I would book a concert, they would ask, "Are you going to do 'I've Just Seen Jesus?'" That got back to management and they came up with an idea to work with the local radio stations to invite local sopranos to "Sing With Larnelle." I fought the idea for a while because I didn't think many people could do the song and do it well. There were some who did do a great job. But they didn't have to! Ultimately, it was a way for us to let people know about the concert and highlight a hometown singer. I finally saw the value in it.

We did the contest for years, hundreds of times. The radio stations would send tapes to the management company from every city scheduled for a concert. We would go through them and choose a soprano. These ladies wanted to either (1) be Sandi for a moment, or (2) sing the song. They were often scared of me. I would say, "It's okay…breathe… You're not Sandi Patty. You want to be the best YOU you can be. All we're going to do tonight is tell the story of Jesus being alive."

We would run through it with the church or community choir backing us up. I spent time rehearsing with the choir. I let them know what they were doing mattered. "We're going to do this together," I told them. "This is your concert." They were my cheerleaders. They were the ticket sellers. They would come up afterwards and say, "Thanks so much for letting me sing with you." We usually sang it three-quarters of the way through the concert. I didn't really introduce the song. I would say, "I did this song with some girl I met. But (hometown girl) is going to come help me tell this wonderful story." I called her name, she came onstage, and the crowd was already on its feet.

The contest was a great way to let people know about the concert and get the community involved. But mainly, people just loved the song. They wanted to hear it. Their hometown girl could not fail. People would come up and say, "Man—she's another Sandi Patty!" I developed a great respect and appreciation for these young women who stepped on stage with me and took on such a big song.

Sandi and I recently re-recorded the duet for my *Larnelle Live in Nashville* DVD/CD. When we first recorded the song, it mostly appeared to be another good career move. But there is not a lyric, a song, an idea I sang back at the beginning of my career that has the same meaning for me then as it does today.

So now, when Sandi and I look at each other and sing particular lines and say those words, I pray to God it's not the same at all. God continues to give weight to words and to songs, and different meanings. There is so much satisfaction in knowing I am continuing to grow.

When Jesus came on the scene and died on the cross, people disputed—and are still disputing—whether those 500 witnesses saw Him resurrected or not. The world is still struggling with that. And if He is alive, He is not the Messiah, some say. "I've Just Seen Jesus" is dealing with some age-old questions mankind still faces.

When Sandi and I sing this song, we typically do it last because it's the home run. We don't put anything after it. What could you put after it? "I've just seen Jesus…I tell you, He's alive!" is a pretty big statement. It is my prayer songs like this bring people to a point of faith by which they can believe Jesus is alive because He rose from the dead, according to the scriptures. And I pray they know all they have done before won't matter anymore because of what He did at Calvary.

"I Miss My Time With You"

In 1986, I was part of a Billy Graham pre-crusade event that gathered all the churches and volunteers together for a concert. I sang my song. I hit every note, meant every word…I heard it all come out of my mouth. There was a standing ovation. But something was missing.

During that time I had been extremely down and didn't really understand the reasons why. I was in one of those funks. So I went to a couple of break-out sessions and prayer services. God has a way of putting us in situations and places where He can work in our lives, and at this event it seemed like everything discussed in the breakout sessions had to do with personal devotion. It was then I understood exactly what was going on—my "first love" had kind of taken a back seat. And I really needed to renew my commitment to a daily walk with Him, which is something I've had to do over and over again.

I came home still feeling empty, but knowing what was missing. I sat at the piano, as I often do when I'm looking for solace and there's no place else to go. I just sat down and put my hands on the keyboard. It wasn't to write anything, I know that. I played this little sequence of chords and started to sing, "I miss my time with you...those moments together..." And everything suddenly came full circle. I thought about those words and realized God had given me the exact thing causing my heart to ache: I was getting into the *business* of singing so much, I had really kind of started doing it by myself.

It was a place where I felt like God was saying to me, *I miss you...I miss YOU. You know those times in the airport when you had your headphones on and you were listening to Me...you were listening to the Word? Where is that? Where is that time when we'd just sit together? You need to know, I miss that.* He was waiting on me because He loved me and missed me, and wanted to impart to me those things that are necessary to my life.

You start to sing something like that and then you can get really wrapped up in your own emotion at that moment. You're playing something and you play it over and over, because you can't move. So you play it again. And then you play it again. And every time, tears are coming. That's how I felt. I spent some time working on what the verses might say and how it might all come together. And I couldn't let it go.

Shortly after that, we were in the studio, recording. I played what I had for Greg Nelson and I think Don Marsh came in and he played it. And then *everybody* heard it—it really came to life. I think Greg knew it was a universal idea. He seemed to know it needed to be heard. But we had to fix the second verse.

So Greg Nelson connected me to Phil McHugh, who wrote "Strength of the Lord." I couldn't wait to work with him because I respected him so much. I believe Ron Harris said in a seminar, "You know, the song's already written…you just have to find it." You have to get yourself out of the way, sweep all the junk away so you can hear, so you can listen and find the song. You must have a propensity for songwriting. But if you do whatever it takes—go to a hotel, go to Maui—get by yourself and sweep it all clean, you'll find it.

Phil and I got together and just did what writers do. We started to pitch ideas, and he gave me great confidence because a lot of the things I was thinking, and some of the ideas and phrases I came up with, he liked! As I spoke, Phil would say, "Yeah, yeah…we can use that." He gave me great confidence because I felt he was a fine writer. He helped me fix the second verse and settle it in.

When you have a song idea, you think, "Well, it's just a little tune. I don't know what it's going to do." It wasn't a hit song to me, it was a lesson. I wasn't thinking, "Wait 'til they hear this! Royalties!" I just knew the idea of the song really helped me on a personal level.

And then it got on the charts because radio station guys and people in the ministry felt they were out there doing everything for the Lord. Busy people would turn on the radio and hear, "When you say you're too busy, busy trying to serve me. Tell me, how can you serve Me, when your spirit's empty? Such a longing in my heart, wanting more than just a part of you…" So, hardworking people doing stuff they think God would want them to do all of a sudden said, "Wait a minute…is this really what I'm supposed to be doing? Am I just busy…busy…working so I have a check, so I have something to do?" It drew people back to a personal, daily relationship with God. And that's what it did for me.

I was a little surprised it did so well because this was a little tune I felt God gave just to me. As the writer, I was afraid it might be ridiculed. I probably had a little of, "Well, I guess it probably won't do very well because it came from me." I'm not a pessimist, but a realist, and I don't always think I have the answer that's going to fix things. I am learning even now God passes things through me and everyone else.

The personal response was tremendous, mostly from people who would say, "It helped me because it talked about the importance of having a daily relationship with God." It's simply like developing a relationship with anyone: You *have* to be with them, you *want* to be with them, you want to know and hear what they have to say about who you are and what you're doing. In this case, God wants to impart daily instructions and blessing and care and comfort to us, because the power to live the life He gives us comes from Him. That information cannot be gleaned anyplace else.

This is something we have all struggled with. I wish I could say that every day I sit down and have a personal relationship with God, a time with Him. Most days I have done that. But during the course of daily living, God brings up something that takes us into a deeper relationship with Him. He allows us, through His love for us, to question His authority over us, His direction, with the very mind He gave us. He's not afraid of the hard questions we ask, the doubts we have, and all of that comes through a relationship with Him.

When I start singing it in concert, the audience starts singing it. It's a thing we all struggle with—personal time we take for granted. We say "Well, if I'm building a multi-million-dollar building for You God, I'm spending time with You. If I'm singing for You—singing loud, singing high, singing cool licks—I'm doing it with You, right?" But God is saying, *That's all very nice, but I want to see you here in the morning because I'll be here.* I had never thought about Him missing me. But He does.

"I Miss My Time With You" went to #1 on the charts, and it really caused many of us in the Christian music industry to consider our busyness—what we were doing and for Whom we were doing it. You can be busy doing a lot of stuff, and none of it has anything to do with the Lord. It has to do with business, with career, with trying to take the next step in your career. Those are not necessarily bad things, but the basis of it all must be that our motivation and ultimate goal is to edify and uplift the Lord.

"Mighty Spirit"

Jerome Olds wrote a small, haunting song for my eleventh album, *I Can Begin Again*, which Greg Nelson again produced. It's a very emotional medley which starts a cappella, "There is a Mighty Spirit…shining out across the sky. He's calling out the weary…to green pastures, come and lie." It's beautiful and poetic with a perfect harmony between music and lyric.

It was never intended to be released as a single. Radio has specific criteria—the song has to be three minutes long and have a beginning where the DJs can talk through it, where they can say, "Good morning!" etc. "Mighty Spirit" wasn't designed that way. I performed it sometimes in concert and just enjoyed it as part of the released album.

But then, as many songs do on a project, it took on a life of its own. It had very little to do with anything we planned. An advertising firm in New York needed a song for a TV campaign and they chose "Mighty Spirit" as the national theme song for President George H.W. Bush's 1993 Points of Light Foundation. "I have spoken of a thousand points of light," Bush said in his 1989 inaugural address, "of all the community organizations that are spread like stars throughout the Nation, doing good."

"Points of Light" is a campaign to shine the light on everyday people who would involve themselves in some of our most pressing issues:

illiteracy, hunger, AIDS, homelessness, gang violence. For example, let's say someone put together a concern, without government funds, to feed people. At the time it was created, President Bush would then "shine the light" on that endeavor in hopes that people may see what could be accomplished without governmental help and thereby inspire other people to start a cause of their own. I was as surprised as everyone when the song became part of the President's Public Service Announcement (PSA) to promote volunteerism.

And then I was thrilled and honored to be invited to the White House to help host meetings where President Bush gave out the Daily Point of Light Award to different volunteers helping their communities solve problems. He honored them for their work, then called on the nation to join them and multiply their efforts. As the President gave the awards, I sang "Mighty Spirit." It was wonderful.

I was just so proud of the White House. I waited in the East Room, then saw him come down the hall. And there were a lot of things going through my mind. *This is probably the most influential person in the world. Coming right here. And who knows who he just got off the phone with, or what he's been dealing with all day?* To stand and watch him as he walked every step. I was glad it took that long for him to walk down the hall, because by the time he got to me, I was pretty settled. But I'm thinking, *Wow! This is the President!* Then he steps out, says, "Hi, Larnelle" and shakes my hand. Now he's George.

The Bushes loved to talk about Michael W. Smith and other Christian artists. In fact, when I met President Bush, he said they listened to Christian music, and they knew me. I went back two or three times after that, so President Bush felt comfortable enough to ask me one time, standing beside the choir, "How do I sound?" He sings bass. I said, "You're doing good!" We had nice little exchanges like that…just George and Larnelle. He was very gracious.

Since then, the Points of Light Foundation has mobilized millions of people through 250 affiliates in 22 countries to solve serious social problems through voluntary service. They're still giving out these awards and President Bush still signs them. In 2013, the White House celebrated the 5,000th Daily Point of Life Award.

In the end, "Points of Light" really launched the tune. It is still part of the longest-running PSA in television history. Someone told me a Detroit radio station used to play it Monday through Friday at 12:00 Noon and hands would just voluntarily reach out and turn up the volume. It's a great lyric, and so many people love it.

The life of "Mighty Spirit" is what it does in concert. It is normally in the line-up after we sing "How Great Thou Art" or another song that's really soul-searching, that really demands attention in a worshipful kind of way. It turns your heart toward worship and praise, and giving glory and honor to the Lord. When Jerome wrote the lyric, "Go tell everybody that love is His command," he never thought past making it a track on the album. No one in the recording studio dreamed the ballad would become a national theme song or part of an international campaign. And I never imagined myself standing in an old Russian church near the

KGB's courtyard, singing "Mighty Spirit" with the choir, watching an old guy shuffling down the aisle like he was a little bit crippled, dressed like a street person. He just kept coming and nobody knew quite what to do. He got to the front, put his arm around my neck and said, "Thank you for coming…thank you for coming…"

That song has opened up so many doors to unexpected places. I'm so happy about that, and I'll never forget them.

"I Can Begin Again"

Dad had not been to the doctor for a long time and some things had caught up to him—some health issues, including sugar diabetes. And he just gave up. The doctors were asking him to give himself shots and he didn't think he could do that. So one day, I went to the doctor with him.

The nurse had to convince Dad to try the shots. You know, injections are mysterious things to somebody who handles plows and bacon. She handed him a syringe and had him inject himself with water. And when he finally did it, he said, "Is that all there is to it?" The inflection in his voice displayed a childlike hope for tomorrow. He could touch tomorrow. And the title came to me: "I can begin again…with the passion of a child."

The lyric, "New beginnings are not just for the young…" was all about my dad at the end of his life. If you take a puppy or a child to visit a nursing home, those residents will find new life because they have got the time and the inclination. They are not thinking, 'I don't have time for this.' They just begin again.

So with the title down, I got serious about finishing the song. I approached John Barker, head of the songwriting division at Benson Records where I was signed as a recording artist at the time. I had a bunch of songs brewing, and was being considered as one of their writers. I said, "John, I really want to understand this process." In the past, I had marveled at Greg Nelson when we would be in the studio and he would say, "That line's weak." And I would read it and say, "Boy, I don't see that…" It wasn't always so apparent. If it was trash, anybody could see it. But Greg knew there was a better word or picture for the second verse. I would hear that and sing it, but I couldn't *see* it. And I wanted to see it. I wanted to learn what a great lyric was. I didn't know very many people who knew how to do that.

John put me with Dave Clark, who has written over 25 #1 Christian songs. I had originally met Dave through a song called "In the Long Run"—just something I was fiddling with, later recorded by contemporary Christian group Truth. Dave was a hit-maker and John knew he could help me with the new song.

So Dave and I met up at a Nazarene church in Bowling Green, Kentucky around Christmas. I said to him, "I don't want you to fix this song. I want you to show me how. I want to know what you're doing." I was a music major. I knew chords and chord structure and conducting. And I knew how to sing. But I didn't understand the craft of writing lyrics—why a line in a song was weak. It rhymed, it cadenced…what's wrong with it? With his help, I began to really understand the process.

We started talking and just ferreting out the idea. I had a melody and a lyric—"I can begin again, with the passion of a child, for my heart has caught a vision of a life that's still worthwhile." I saw all that in my dad's face. And then, "Alone again in a crowded room…" Who hasn't felt that? You are by yourself, the room is full and you're just wandering around, and you can't hear anybody. You should feel companionship and brotherhood, but you don't. Dave and I met a few more times and worked through every element of the song.

I was more than a little surprised at the response when I started working it into concerts. I've always had a real pull toward a more soulful medley with a bit of jazz flavor. But my audience expects anthems, and I've always felt I had to be careful. Because when I go into a place to sing, I want the crowd to think they will hear one kind of music all night long in order to relate and have a worship experience. Although "I Can Begin Again" has a pop/jazz vibe, people wanted to hear it.

It surprised me because I thought I knew my audience. I'm careful and concerned about the audience. I'm always watching out for them. I don't want to do anything to leave them out of the experience, which means I don't always do everything I personally want to do. It's probably without merit. I'm finding more places are opening up to all kinds of things. I started doing "I Can Begin Again," and some of the older crowd started asking for it because they related to the lyric. They tell me it was a new beginning for them. There's usually a story behind it: I lost my mom, or I had to change jobs. They had to start something again they thought was impossible. A 50-year-old trying to be retrained for a job. That's a tough thing. Losing a loved one, a child. Very tender stories. There is no change like starting over, having to make a decision because you've been laid off from your job. You feel like maybe you're too late for college, you're too late to be trained for something. And yet you get out there and some intuitive nurse has you give yourself a shot in the leg and you say, "You know what? I can do that."

What's interesting is while the lyrics never mention God or Jesus by name, the Christian experience is implied, transcending race, nationality, and age group, where "new beginnings are not just for the young." It's designed to be uplifting and hopeful.

I don't know if I ever told Dad it was a tribute song to him. I'm not sure he ever heard me sing it live. But I think he would have been appreciative knowing he was the inspiration.

"Teach Me to Love"

In 1994, Randy Phillips, then-president of Promise Keepers, asked Steve Green and I to write a song about one of the "Seven Promises of Promise Keepers," specifically: *A Promise Keeper is committed to reaching beyond any racial and denominational barriers to demonstrate the power of biblical unity.*" They wanted a racial-reconciliation song, based on our life experiences. Steve was raised in a small village in Argentina as the only white-skinned, fair-haired kid in an entire town of indigenous people. I had some instances of prejudice during high school and traveling with the Spurrlows. We both had practical research to channel into a song.

Many people thought the song was necessary, and I agreed with it. A lot of the racial stuff hit the fan in the 60s, and a lot of us—both black and white—moved to the suburbs and never took the opportunity to stick around and deal with that unpleasantness. A lot of the guys who came to Promise Keepers were of an age that fit into that category. They simply had not dealt with it. It wasn't that they were even outwardly expressing any views of prejudice at all, and probably from a distance loved everyone. And yet, sometimes when you haven't come face to face with something—or lived with it for a while, or have a relationship with someone—you really don't understand or know what you feel, because you haven't explored it at all.

So Steve and I walked through the process of exploring the past to write a song for the present. We never got into the same room to write the song, but we labored together over the idea on many occasions, discussing different concepts. Then, Phil Naish wrote some great music. Phil was the studio keyboard player for Steve, Sandi Patty, Dolly Parton and worked with Steven Curtis Chapman. He did a wonderful job.

I wrote the first verse because I understood the lyric, "All my life I've had to struggle to be free." There were a number of instances of being on the wrong end of someone hating or not wanting to be around me simply because of color. There were times in the Spurrlows when we would be ministering in some churches or working with Christian people putting on a concert and the black kids in the group would have to stay in a hotel, separately. Of course, we thought that was pretty cool because we had a swimming pool and room service. But it was, by and large, because the church bylaws in some instances stated they could not have people of color in their church. It was very troubling.

Steve wanted his verse to talk about asking for forgiveness for years of thinking from a "white," non-person-of-color perspective—the permeating idea that you're less if you're a person of color and you're better if you're not. It's a challenging lyric and exactly what the Promise Keepers staff wanted to recognize to make sure this issue was dealt with.

Promise Keepers was an unusual meeting for men, coming together for something other than a sporting event to deal with some real life issues. It would have been a great tragedy had we not dealt with this issue. It's certainly not as important as the salvation of one's soul or growing in Christ, but it's an issue Christian men especially needed to deal with. If you want to change a man, you don't do it by grabbing him by the collar and shaking him and asking him about his soul, smacking him across the face, or getting in gun battles or fisticuffs or word wars. You change a man by changing his heart.

Promise Keepers events always had large numbers of attendees—40,000 to 60,000 men. It was amazing. We sang "Teach Me To Love" under the banner of "Break Down the Walls" in a number of these enormous events. "Love your brother as yourself" was not a new idea, but the song reminded us we needed to think about it on a deeper level. I can say that because I went through the exercises of writing it, singing it and listening to it, it brought about questions in me. I'm here with 50,000 men to praise God. But do I love that guy over there? In reckless abandon? Do I really love this black guy? Do I really love this white guy? Do I really love this Hispanic guy? Do I really love this Polish guy? Do I really? I hope it brought about those kinds of responses in the people who heard the song as well.

After the events, I got comments like, "I really never thought of this before," which was directly in line with the goal. We harbor things we don't even know we have. There were some men in tears who would be dreadfully sorry they had any inkling of racism in their hearts. I remember an altar call regarding racial reconciliation and thousands of men coming to the altar to pray about this. I remember walking around in the audience, praying with different guys. I knew, even having been a Christian for many years, I still harbored some of that stuff in my heart. And I probably still do because I'm not perfect. But I'm constantly working on it, constantly heading in the right direction.

Love calls on you to do things you don't want to do sometimes. It calls on you to care for people you wouldn't typically want to care for. It causes you to go fishing with folks you don't want to be around. Love is the overriding theme—the mysterious, wonderful, life-changing agape love. And that's what God calls us to. That is not our normal default, but when the corruptible becomes the incorruptible, it will be. Everything else will pass away, but love will remain.

The real key to this message is: What does that do in your life tomorrow? What does it do on a daily basis in your life? Does it cause you to think? Does it cause you to change? Repenting from sin is to turn, to be born again is to turn around. It means to turn in a different direction, walk in a new direction. And every once in a while, because I'm human, I look back. I'm so thankful that pillar-of-salt thing is over with. But sometimes, I look over my shoulder from where I have been. I remind myself to look forward, look away from the old person I was. Every once in a while, we look back and get a glimpse because we are human. But not for long. And not long enough to take us back to where we were, where we began this process.

The song has very special meaning to me because we think we know how to love and we find out we don't. We find out every day we have absolutely no idea. And so, I look to the Heavens, I raise my hands, continually, daily, renewing that request—Lord, teach me to love. It's an ongoing process. I missed it today. I insulted someone because I thought they were going to insult me. "So Lord, on a daily basis, teach me to love." The Scripture says, "If you don't love your brother whom you see every day, then how can you love Me?" The evidence that I love God first depends on loving the people I'm here with on earth every day, trying to make life better for them.

Being with people of different races or ethnicities is not an occasion to build a wall, but it affords us the opportunity to learn other cultures and how someone else thinks or feels. When we go through that process, we usually find out we are more alike than we ever were different.

"Amen"

In 1987, Greg Nelson needed one more song for my next album. He found it in a new arrangement of an old, old Negro spiritual written by Jester Hairston. I had heard "Amen" many times—Sidney Poitier got an Oscar for it in 1963's *Lilies of the Field*, The Impressions made it popular, then it went through many transformations in genres from gospel to Otis Reddings' R&B to funk. It wasn't a song I had even considered recording, but some friends of mine considered it. So I began to listen to it and discovered not only was it fun, but it has within its simple lyric the entire gospel story. Little baby in the manger—that's where it starts. Christ crucified, and then He rose on Easter. So it's a very hopeful kind of lyric. I got quite excited about recording it.

The next step was finding a fresh arrangement for my voice. We had several discussions with arranger Alan Moore about laying out the chords and form, and he began to put little elements in there specifically for my voice. Some people have a knack for giving songs a little twist, and his arrangement woke up the song for me. Now it had heft and I just loved singing it. At first, I didn't care for the original middle part where it just drops down, drops out. But Alan said, "Trust me." And when the orchestra got there and started playing those chords, well… Alan had molded the music of the middle part into a minor key where the lyric talks about Christ being crucified, and you think about the cross and the cruelty of the cross, and all that Christ endured because of His great love for us. It gets low and sad. Then suddenly it bursts out into victory after that section…major key! "But He rose on Easter!"

The melody of "Amen" is not an easy song, as it's been crafted. It is what we term a "singer's song." From a vocal point of view, it lets me do all those little things that aren't very common to do. It's a dynamic vocal exercise. Sometimes I like to sing background. I've been in many choirs and madrigal groups, and it's good to rejoice together with deep, rich chords. So the melodic exercise, the choir, the killer arrangement, the orchestra—it was all terrific. If a song goes where I expect it to go, it doesn't do anything for me. When I heard it in its original form, it didn't. But when I heard the new arrangement, it was me.

The crafting of the song is designed to get into your head, so you're singing, "Amen…Amen…" and you don't even know it. When you get into a business meeting, you want to get people saying, "Yes…yes…" That song says, "Yes…Amen…yes, yes!" *So be it.* That's what it means. Great word. *Amen*, Jesus died for me. *Amen*, He's the beginning and the end. *Amen*, He is worthy of our praise.

God's Word has a way of sneaking up on you. So while you're singing along, you are getting something else. Your mind and body and spirit are totally separate things here. My body needs to snap or clap or dance along to the music. My spirit just needs to drink. And if we believe God's Word never leaves us and does what it's supposed to do, then we know the story of the Gospel has done what it's supposed to do. You're reacting to the high note at the end, but your spirit is reacting to the whole Gospel story you just heard. It's saying, "yes…yes…"

It was never released as a single because it's an up-tempo song, but the audience found it. You have to have "moments" in a concert. You have to have different "moods." When I started singing it live, people started loving it and singing it with me, and I started ending the program with it. It's one of the most requested songs I do. I enjoy it every time I sing it.

But it's done something else for me. It's taught me: Be careful what you're famous for. Try not to sing any junk, because you'll be stuck singing it forever. So, I've been very, very thankful it's become a signature tune.

The Awards

When I was nominated for the first Grammy in 1984, I sat in the corner of my house and thought, *Wow…somebody's listening to my songs!* And then I went to Los Angeles and won it. I could hardly believe it, and I couldn't wait to share it with my family. I got home the next day, walked into the house and before I could even think about getting a big head from my big accomplishment, I found this note stuck to the fridge:

Larnelle,
Congrats on the Grammys…we're proud of you.
I'm off to school. Be sure to set the garbage out.
Don't forget the cans in the garage.
Love ya, M

That's Mitzy—keeping it real! I just laughed and laughed. I still have that note. It's a wonderful reminder every time a "recognition" comes my way that an award is just one moment in time, but the real stuff has to be taken care of every day.

I have had mixed feelings about awards over the years. On one hand, it is gratifying to be recognized for working hard in my field of expertise. At the beginning of my career, any kind of benchmark notice was helpful to book concerts and work with talented people. But what I didn't think about—at all—was that when I "won," someone else "lost." Part of human nature is that the person who loses out on the award doesn't do well, and the person who wins often thinks too much of himself or herself. At the 1984 Grammys, I was up against Mylon LeFevre & Broken Heart, the Gaither Vocal Band, the Imperials, Masters V, and White Heart—all terrific groups, all very deserving of being recognized for their music. But after winning my fifth Grammy, I began to be on the losing end and started questioning my music, and comparing myself to the winners.

The Bible warns us against comparing ourselves to others, and the famous writer Mark Twain summed it up this way: "Comparison is the death of joy." So when I really wanted to be miserable, I started to compare myself to people that seemingly everything they touched turned to gold. If only I had sold 50 trillion recordings…if only I could play the piano like that, or sing like that, or talk like that… And when that was too miserable, I searched for someone who was not doing as well as me—maybe someone who wasn't even nominated—with the catch being that I was then rejoicing over their failures. It's an ugly, ugly process, and I struggled with it all the time.

Years ago, God started taking me through this minefield and taught me some valuable lessons—part of my "growth package" I use to this day. Before a particular event, I get a list of every artist in that event, on the campus, performing or giving a seminar, and I spend the next few months in my own quiet time, praying for each person. As I sit in the audience after weeks of prayer, I find it very, very difficult to compare myself to them. Even more, I enjoy what they have to say and how God is using them! I am able to listen and be deeply moved by their words and music. What they are doing encourages me even more so to be the best I can be for the Lord. It's not until the entire event is over and I'm on my way home that I realize what's happened: Because I took my own issues and laid them at the cross of Christ, the unguarded response was simply to be blessed. I was actually and mysteriously vested in each person, egging them on as though our lives and ministries were interwoven. Rather than feeling jealousy, I was overjoyed in the message God had brought through them. What a revelation!

Every time I go through the same process. Every. Single. Time. If I don't, I come home depressed and wanting to be someone other than me. And if I am caught up in being someone else, who is being me? My goal and prayer is to be the very best me I can be. That's what God requires of me—to rest in Him and have joy for everything He does through my brothers and sisters who are honoring Him. That frees me to do my very best in representing Him, as though it is the last time I may have the chance to do so.

There is really only one person we're called to be like, and I used to sing a song about that in the Spurrlow concerts: "I Want to be More Like Jesus Every Day." That's how the Gospel reaches out and touches people. I will reach people with my ministry who no one else can reach. And my brothers and sisters will reach others I could never reach. That unites us in the goal of going into every crevice and every corner to preach and share the Gospel of Jesus Christ.

Chapter 8

GOD IS COLOR BLIND

I have been to some of the most beautiful places in the world. From the beautiful landscape of Alaska to the rolling hills of Europe to the raw outback of Africa, I have seen God's handiwork all over the world. God is certainly NOT color blind, in fact, His creation proves how much He truly loves a colorful canvas. And the children's song we used to sing in Sunday School is still true – "red and yellow, black and white, we are precious in His sight."

I used to make a bold statement in concert, and probably need to go back to saying it again. When it comes to seeing different races of people, God is as color blind as He can be. There was a time in our country—and still is, really—when people acted like they didn't know that. And this goes beyond just being the "different kid" in the 60s, the "Whites Only" bathrooms, or getting forced off the sidewalk. Even those of us who are Christians need to be reminded from time to time of God's colorblindness.

I don't particularly like to revisit the past, dredging up slights and wrongs and a legacy of international segregation in music. But I went there for a song Steve Green and I did together called "Teach Me to Love," and I'm going there now. Racial prejudice needs to be discussed. It needs absolution.

Our School Activist

Miss Helen Fisher, our Bate School librarian, gave me my first taste of civil disobedience when I was just a teen. She gathered some of us up and marched us into a restaurant across the street from the school for a sit-in. We went in, sat at the counter, and ordered some lunch. We were not evicted or arrested, no one dumped ketchup on us or attacked us. The staff waited on us after a time and it was fine. What I didn't know then was Miss Fisher was the first president of the Danville chapter of the NAACP and would have considered sit-ins not only educational, but a move toward making real change in our nation. She was called into the school office later and chastised for it, but she insisted student sit-ins were part of her citizenship rights and, really, an obligation.

See, Miss Fisher grew up with parents who were denied anything higher than a 6th-grade education. She had fought for her three degrees—fought through segregated schools, limited classes and extension work because of race, dorm room assignments by the furnace or hot water heater, and being ignored in class. She fought until she was the first black woman to receive a Master of Arts in Library Science from the University of Kentucky.

She gave an oral history interview in 2000 in which she stated, "I believe in the Fatherhood of God, the Brotherhood of Man, and I am an integrationist." And this was after she had retired from teaching in 1980. Feisty even into her 90s, she reminded me that sit-ins helped her—and her students—develop an attitude that those who put others down are the individuals to feel truly sorry for. And that mindset, that training, became critical during one incident on the road.

A Change of Heart

Traveling with the Spurrlows, I was one of only four black kids in the group. I didn't think about that much until after a college concert in Arkansas.

After a full day of performing, the entire group went to a restaurant for dinner. We took our seats and sat there for the longest time. Nobody waited on us or even gave us menus. We thought they were just busy. So, some of the kids got up, found some menus, passed them out… just helping out. We were a big group that had descended on a small restaurant. We wanted to be polite.

We kept sitting there until the owner appeared and stood in the middle of the floor. "You guys have to leave," he said. "I cannot have niggers and whites eating together in my restaurant." We just looked at him in shocked silence, then got up and walked out. This was in the 1970s. That kind of statement was becoming a very ancient, tired, ridiculous-sounding rhetoric, even at that point.

The owner followed us out of his restaurant, along with some other patrons who were standing behind him, backing him up. Now, I didn't see this man take a drink, but it was apparent from his voice and flushed face that he probably had found some "liquid courage" to confront us. I immediately sensed this was becoming a very, very volatile situation, like a tinderbox that was about to be lit and catch fire.

Thurlow Spurr, our leader, was with us and stepped forward to argue the absurdity of this stance. Then I stepped forward to stop Thurlow. When I did that, the owner pointed his finger at me and said, "I wouldn't hurt that kid for anything in the world." Well, his stance and his body language were saying totally the opposite. "But I cannot," he said with such fervency it was almost like a sermon, almost like a declaration, "I cannot allows blacks and whites to eat together in my restaurant."

And at that moment, I think I dealt with a lot of my own prejudices, my own hate, because I think I started to see it as something else. I started to see that hate was a nasty, dirty emotion that does little more than raise your blood pressure and shorten your life. When I heard that man's words, I heard the hate, but it had something else to it: fear—a lack of understanding, even a lack of education. When I heard him speak, Miss Fisher's training rang in my ears and I started to feel sorry for him. Every time he spoke, I tried to understand a little bit more. And I think at that point, I began to deal with the deep-seated racial issues I didn't even know I had.

I think it was more evidence that God was working in my heart. Because when that man lashed out at us and those words began to take shape in front of him, obviously I didn't care for the person created from those words. But it wasn't like I wanted to strike back at him. Miss Fisher and the grace of God spoke into my heart, and started changing my heart.

Now, that wasn't the end of it. That night, we all stayed in a hotel and up and down the street, all night long, we could hear trucks speeding by. We were told the FBI was called and they somehow made certain our hotel was being protected. This was a good-old-boy stance against something the restaurant owner and his friends felt was a threat. We left the next morning.

Years later, I went back to that college town and did a concert there at a church. I found out that after we told the Little Rock Bureau of Racial Relations what happened, the restaurant was closed—went out of business or was put out of business. I didn't mention the long-ago incident, and yet I felt something. I felt that old stuff kind of brewing up again. I felt that old awareness of walking into a store to buy a shirt or some toothpaste and waiting, ready for somebody to say something negative. And you know what? There are times I still feel a little bit of that.

But that night at the church, it would have served no purpose to talk about that old situation with its past attitudes and prejudices. It would have done no good to beat up on those people who weren't even there in the 70s, had nothing to do with the confrontation, and make them relive it for guilt or shock or any other reason. What purpose was served was leading those folks in worship, rejoicing in the Lord who does indeed bring about change in our hearts by the Holy Spirit.

God calls upon us to forgive and forget. I forgave right away, but I'll never forget that night in Arkansas. I don't have the ability to do that. But the evidence was plain that God was still working in my heart.

Breaking Down Walls Through Music
I believe God puts us where He needs us. Sometimes He calls on us to "run to the roar"—run toward the challenge instead of away from it. I am a black artist with widespread appeal to white audiences. That's not something I set out to do, but I believe God stationed me there. I am not ashamed of that and feel no different from any other artist of any race. But I do consider the opportunities I have had to bring racial integration into the gospel music world as part of God's call on my life.

In music—even in Christian music—there are not many black artists in certain areas of the industry. I have had the privilege of performing in settings where black gospel artists had rarely been featured. Sometimes I would run into people with the mindset that because I'm black, there are certain sounds, certain things I should sing. I remember when I started in the gospel music business, Andraé Crouch—pastor and gospel singer famous for songs like "Through It All" and "Let the Church Say Amen"—was a popular artist, selling lots of records. And it seemed in the industry's opinion, if you were black, you needed to sound like that. But I learned early on, God had given me a specific gift and the courage to be the Larnelle He had made. The audience wouldn't have believed me if I had tried to sound like everyone else. I needed to do what I felt God had called me to do and settle into that.

I had a black couple tell me a story some years ago. They were lying in bed, listening to the radio, when they heard my song "Friends in High Places" start to play. They both describe being whisked up in the music and the message, and sitting up in bed to hear it better. When the song was over, the lady exclaimed (not knowing who the singer was), "Boy, that white boy can sing!" I laughed when they told me this story, but it makes a great point: If we can all get to a place where we shut the eyes of our old prejudices or fears, and just listen—really listen—to what God is saying through His word and His Spirit, we would truly be moved by the message of hope and love, and we won't care where it comes from.

Recently, I was invited to the Kentucky State Capitol in Frankfort to receive an honor. I was signing some autographs after the award ceremony when someone came up and asked, "Do you remember me?" It took me back for a moment. I did remember him. My mom was friends with his family's maid, Miss Hattie. I remember going to the big house where Miss Hattie worked, but only visiting one part of the home. There were parts of the house where we didn't—where we couldn't—go. This man, who was standing in front of me under the giant dome of the Kentucky State Capitol, had been the little boy in the "other" part of the house. As children, we couldn't play together because there were many walls keeping us apart. But that day, when we met again, there was no wall at all. We were standing eye-to-eye, smiling and hugging and sharing stories. I mentioned Miss Hattie and he began to cry, remembering her as a treasured person in his life as she had been in mine. Time has a wonderful way of healing memories and correcting old wrongs.

Like many people of color, discrimination was, and often still is, a part of my daily life. And I, like others, will always confront such issues with the love and compassion my faith demands. It is my hope that those of us who are called by the name of Christ will be in the forefront of stamping out the notion that no person, regardless of race, creed or color, is better than another.

Chapter 9

FAMILY TIME

Everyone's story begins and ends with family, and mine is no different. My immediate and extended families have been so important in shaping who I am as a son, brother, nephew, cousin, husband, father and grandfather. They were—and still are—critical to my life and career, lessons and message. As we come full circle in this narrative, here are a few more memories.

Parenting on Purpose

When the nurse held up to the viewing window, first Lonnie, then four years later, Teresa, and said, "Here's your son…here's your daughter," I was overwhelmed. My heart was so tender, I cried—both times. Those were moments I realized God used the love between Mitzy and me to bring these beautiful babies into the world.

Early on, I was away on a tour and was gone quite a while, more than a couple of weeks at a time. I got home and I remember going into Lonnie's room and looked at him as he slept. He was longer and was getting thicker, getting bigger, growing. It began to dawn on me right then: this growth process was going to happen faster than I realized. It wouldn't be long before he would be walking and then in grade school, then high school, then college. I knew I had to begin making tough choices about my career. Often, I was invited to participate in important events, but if it coincided with Thanksgiving or Christmas, or one of my children's birthdays or a special moment in their lives, I chose my kids. I would sometimes get a bit of push-back from industry folks who believed I was missing out on growing my career, but I understood something very important after battling the loss of my voice: Singing may go away tomorrow, but I was going to be a father for the rest of my days, and I wanted to make that the priority in my life.

Mitzy and I had decided early in our relationship we would rather be with each other than anybody else we knew. Except for a few occasions, we stayed as true as we could to that. We wanted to make certain that at any given moment our children understood Mom and Dad wanted to be with them.

So we started to pray about that and God laid something on my heart I have never forgotten. I felt the Lord was saying to me, *I'll get you where I need you. You will miss some things those around you think are pretty important and you should not miss. There will be some career moves those around you will insist you should take. I will pick which ones you should take. I will lay that on your heart.* I trusted God in that. And I am certain I missed opportunities other people may have jumped at the chance to do. But as I look back, we have loosed two young people into the world who I am very, very, very proud of. So, whatever I missed was worth it.

Our son, Lonnie, was our little entrepreneur and inventor early on. He was always coming up with things to build and ways to make money. He was about five years old when he rolled a huge stump in a wagon into our garage and announced he was going to make a slingshot. Now, my first impulse was to say, "You can't do that! Look at that huge stump! Let me help you." But I refrained. I simply handed him the tools and let him go. Thankfully, he didn't cut off his arm or anything, but it helped me realize my job was to guide, protect and provide, then to stand back when needed and allow my kids to grow into the people they were going to be.

He decided he wanted a paper route when he was around 12. I had a paper route at that age and I didn't do it very long. I got tired of getting up early—often in the rain—having to collect money that many of the customers never seemed to have, and so forth. So I knew what he was signing up for. "Your job, your responsibility," I told him. That was, until the day one of his customers called and said he didn't get the paper. Lonnie had already gone to school, so what did I do? Well, I grabbed a paper out of his stash and I delivered it to his customer…in my newly-purchased Mercedes. I'm sure the neighbors saw my car and thought delivering papers might be a pretty good job opportunity!

Later on, Lonnie decided he wanted to do some lawn work for our neighbors. Mitzy had to take him because he was too young to drive, and she couldn't stand to watch him do it by himself so she would get out of the car and help him with the yard work. Sometimes, if he was running late or needed extra help, we would all pile into the car and go cut lawns. There we were—a Grammy winner, a teacher with a Master's degree in special education, our gymnast daughter flipping all over the yard, and Lonnie—all out in the neighborhood mowing and trimming lawns. But it was moments like that I hope my kids will always remember—that mom and dad were willing to do *anything* to support them and spend time with them.

Now, Teresa was our adventurer. If Lonnie was our rule-follower, Teresa was our rule-*bender*. One time, I was on the road and Mitzy called me late at night, rather frantic. She said someone had been messing with our boat in the back yard and had climbed into it. She wanted to know if she should call the police. I said, "How do you know someone is in the boat?" to which she replied, "Teresa saw him from the roof." Well, the boat intruder suddenly became unimportant as I exclaimed, "What in the world is Teresa doing on the roof?" She'd apparently found a ladder I had laid against the back of the house and decided to take a trip to our rooftop to look at the stars.

One day in elementary school, Teresa's teacher asked the kids to talk about what kind of work their parents did. Teresa said, "My dad doesn't work." The teacher said, "Well, he must work, Teresa. You have nice clothes and shoes. I am sure he works." To which Teresa replied, "No, he doesn't work. He sings." She didn't really think what I did was a career! Both my kids had musical talent. Teresa was a great singer and drummer, and Lonnie was terrific on the saxophone. But I never pushed them into music careers or offered to put them on stage. I knew how fickle the music business could be, but mostly I wanted them to find their own ways in life.

One of Mitzy's philosophies in parenting, and one I agreed with, was "the answer is always 'no' first." Whatever the question, the answer was "no." If we said "no" to something they wanted to do and they didn't complain, everything was fine. But if they challenged us on it, the initial "no" gave us time to think about it and consider how important it was to them. Sometimes we would change the answer, but the first answer was always "no." When the kids were in high school and there was a party or an overnight activity, Lonnie and Teresa had learned by then not to even bring the idea home. They knew what the answer would be.

We had tough boundaries, but we always let our kids know why. We wanted them to know the discipline in our house was nothing compared to what they would experience on the "street." We stressed to them that the lessons they would learn out in the world would be much tougher than any discipline they got from us. We loved them. The world didn't. And our rules were set in place because of our love for them and our desire to protect them.

Mitzy and I believed *quality* time had a lot to do with *quantity* time, so I did my best to be home at least two Sundays out of each month and to limit long tour spans. But sometimes, the phone had to suffice. I often had to step in with some discipline via a phone call with the kids. I remember one time I was talking with Lonnie and he wanted to talk about his faith. I could tell he was seeking the Lord and needing to talk through his salvation. It was a moment I would have preferred to have been sitting with him on the couch, looking into his eyes, but I was also thankful distance didn't keep me from sharing the moment with him.

Today, our kids have kids of their own. They have promising careers and are married to wonderful people. They live close by so they stop in often, sometimes just to talk about work or ask us some parenting advice. We are so thankful we have that kind of relationship with them. We realize God allowed us to have them for a while, and our singular prayer was always, "Lord, help us not to mess them up." God answered that prayer.

Another Calling

I spent much of my childhood going to a holiness church near our home. Those were some interesting and fun services. Mom would get happy, praising the Lord, and would dance and shout. You don't see that much these days. I guess we have become a bit sophisticated and high-churched for that kind of worship. But at this church, it was standard practice, prompted by the Spirit. Mom and those other saints would dance and shout for joy in the Lord. It was infectious and real. Even at a tender age, I was aware something special was going on at these meetings and with these people. It wasn't too long before I joined the First Baptist Church not far from there. They had a good youth program and my school principal's wife was in charge of the youth choir. I guess even at a young age, I was trying to find my own way, my own faith.

It seemed natural when some years later Mom and Dad moved their membership to the church I had joined. It was great being there together. Eventually, Dad became a deacon in our church. He would go pray with the pastor, visit the sick, and lean on his own tough experiences and sense of humor to counsel others. I observed all this as a teenager and benefited from wisdom passed down visually. I saw Dad's hard-won wisdom in action.

So it shouldn't have been a surprise when decades later I was asked to be a church deacon. I never would have volunteered or sought it out, but I'm certainly glad God hemmed me in so I would seriously consider it. In fact, this was a calling and I knew it. Somehow I knew this was an area of ministry I needed to explore and, probably at the end of it all, it would give me more insight for my ministry as a whole.

I didn't think I had the age and experience and wisdom Dad had as a deacon, so I turned to scripture to get a handle on what being a deacon was all about.

Now this was the beginning of a whole other area and level of service in my heart, whether I became a deacon or not. Every great evangelist, every singer, every church employee, Sunday School worker, or church bus driver really has one job: That the Word of God be spread. We want to serve people in such a way they will want to hear the Word we demonstrate as we minister to them.

So I became a deacon, just like my dad. And I quickly learned how thankful I was for the people who had spoken into my life over the years: the Danville community, the teachers and grandmas and aunts and people who cared and supported everything good in my young life, people who in an unselfish way—not wanting or expecting anything—cared for me.

I started caring that same way for others. It is hard to sit with a family who has had a tragedy, and want to say something to fix it. It is a helpless feeling. It's often not the time to encourage or counsel with scripture. If I could, I would take the pain on myself. But I have learned I can be there to comfort them without saying a word. They appreciate the gesture in silence.

I heard a story one time that has stuck with me for many years and has been really important in my service as a deacon. The story goes like this: There was a little girl who showed up to her class quite late one morning. This was very unusual for her and her teacher was interested in what had happened to make her late. She explained to her teacher she was late because her best friend Sally had broken her doll. Though this was unfortunate, the teacher still didn't see this as a good excuse for being late to class. So the teacher inquired further, "Well, did you help her fix it?" She said, "No I couldn't help her fix it, I just helped her cry." I wrote a song about that story entitled "I'll Help You Cry." It shows that we don't always have the right words, but God will use our presence in the lives of others to minister to them in times of need.

Saying Goodbye

Except for that one dark year of incarceration, Dad was a daily part of our lives. All the grandparents got to see Lonnie and Teresa grow up. Mitzy's parents lived across the field from us and my parents were 80 miles away. I'm so happy the kids got to know their grandparents, but I'm even happier they got to experience the inevitable process of life winding down.

My mother had a series of health problems during her lifetime and passed away before Dad. At the time of her death, she and Dad had been married 50 years. She was a strong, determined lady who wouldn't even think of going to the hospital until she had put on the proper clothes.

Dad was even tougher. After he retired, he bought a little hobby farm with cows and a small garden. He cut himself with a chain saw once and nearly bled to death as he drove himself to the hospital. He later encountered other health issues and it was difficult for him to accept not being able to do things he had always done. Our kids were teenagers when Dad's health began to deteriorate. As a teen, you look at life and think things will go on, just as they are, forever. All our kids had ever seen were grandparents who were healthy and vibrant and ready to go and do things with them.

But sometimes when we would bring Dad home from dialysis, he wouldn't be able to get up the steps. Lonnie and Theresa had never seen that before. And once again, Dad was teaching us something. God was using these health problems to teach our kids that life has its ups and downs. Things don't go right all the time. Life throws some unpleasant things at you, and you must deal with them.

Bill and Gloria Gaither wrote a song about not wanting everything to go right all the time. They wished their kids some difficult times and heartache, because that's part of life. Our parents were teaching our kids, whether they knew it or not, that life has some painful changes. And part of that pain is saying goodbye.

My parents wanted me to be the best adult I could be. To be honest, I'm still working on that. They wanted me to be a good person. That is still my goal. Every early dark moment my parents experienced, combined with the light of their later years, made them wonderful examples to me. Their legacy still remains in my heart.

Chapter 10

PAST IS PROLOGUE

J esus was only 12 years old when he walked into the temple and began to preach. His frantic parents finally found him and I'm sure said what most of us have when we have lost sight of our child for a few minutes, "Where were you? What were you thinking?" Jesus simply replied, "'But why did you need to search?' he asked. 'Didn't you know that I must be in my Father's house?'" (NLT)

A few years ago, Dave Clark, Danny Bunnelle and I wrote a song about that exchange simply entitled "Didn't You Know?" and recorded it with the Brooklyn Tabernacle Choir. It is a difficult song for me to sing because there are a lot of emotions that come bubbling up to the surface. As I have reflected on all the people who have poured into my life, it is as if I can hear them all saying in one way or the other, "Didn't you know what you were supposed to be doing? Didn't you recognize God's hand in your life?"

I now understand why Mr. Summers took me into his office and sang to me. It was his way of saying, "Don't you realize—in spite of what anyone else says—it is ok to be a boy soprano?" I now know what Miss Georgie was saying when she took me, often reluctantly, to sing for all the tea parties, churches, and group meetings—"Don't you know, Larnelle, that you have been given a gift from God and you need to share it with everyone?"

There is a doctrine in Christian theology called Typology which is the study of the types of Christ in the Old Testament. Moses, Elijah, Abraham are a few of the people who mirrored aspects of the Messiah who was yet to come. In reality, that is our commission as Christians. We are all to be types of Christ to the people around us. We are to be His hands and feet to the people within our sphere of influence. This journey has made me appreciate, even more, the people who did that— who were that—to me.

I remember working on my first album, and we were rehearsing vocals for the song "Lord, Listen to your Children Praying." The producer, Bergen White, hit the Record button and I started singing. He stopped suddenly and said, "No, no. Sing it like you did before. *Do what you just did.*" I wasn't sure what that meant, but I just kept singing and he kept stopping. After that, he told his engineer to keep the Record button on all the time, even during rehearsals. While writing this book, I have hit the Rewind and Replay buttons a lot. I have had to endure the pain all over again of mistakes I made, of things left unsaid, of the loss of family and friends. But I have also observed that a lot of good advice and counsel from many talented, caring people was transferred to me, and I have done my best to emulate their wisdom over the course of my life. I have tried to do what they did, the way they did it. And like them, I have attempted to pay it forward, offering the same knowledge, compassion, encouragement, and support to the people in my life—in my sphere of influence. I hope my life has become a song they will always enjoy hearing—and I pray I recorded it exactly the way God wanted me to sing it.

Afterword

MEANWHILE, OFF-STAGE...

I am not an international man of mystery, but I confess to having a few aliases.

If you knew me in the early 70s and had a Citizens' Band (CB) radio, my "handle" was Mr. Music. If we got acquainted after the late 70s and you had a ham radio license, you might have called me "Stu" or even WD4LZC. And you would have given me a shout-out in Morse code.

That's right—in addition to the French and German and Elizabethan love songs I had to learn as a voice major at WKU, I soon tasked myself to learn American CB slang for short distances, then entered the world of ham radio to communicate with people all over the world in a universal language.

"10-4, Mr. Music. Watch your back door."

Although the CB radio service began in 1945, it really gained popularity in the late-60's with radio clubs and truckers and its own slang language. I had a CB radio in my home and if a "good buddy" called me on it using my handle "Mr. Music…" I might be on the air for a long time.

And then the CB culture exploded after the 1973 oil crisis and nationwide 55 mph speed limit. Suddenly, we all needed to know where the best-priced gasoline was, where the police were, and what the truckers were up to. I had installed a CB in my car and a three-fool antenna on the trunk, and I could work that slang and 10-code ("10-4" or "OK, message received, " "what's your 20") with the best of them. Smokey and the Bandit had nothing on us.

Then I met some radio operators who were involved a radio spectrum I had heard of, but knew very little about. It was called amateur radio, better known as ham radio. The basic tenant of this area of radio was, and is, community service.

One of the guys, a pastor friend of mine, invited me to his home to see his setup. I've often heard it said that presentation is everything, and in this case, it worked. I showed up at his home. He guided me to a little dark room; we walked in and at just the right moment he hit a switch and all these different radios lit up like a Christmas tree. I was enthralled. There in front of me in all their glory were transmitters, amplifiers and switches. There were maps on the walls with color pins denoting the states and countries he had been able to contact on antennas made from a few pieces of wire. Yes, I was definitely hooked. Message received.

The next day, I was gathering together the materials that I would need to study in order to get my amateur radio licenses under the watchful eye of the Federal Communications Commission. The biggest hurdle would be the required sending and receiving of Morse code. It is a series of short and long electrical pulses developed in the 1830s and 1840s by Samuel Morse (1791-1872) and other inventors. The telegraph revolutionized long-distance communication. It worked by transmitting signals over a wire laid between stations, or antenna to antenna through the air waves using a telegraph key. I had never seen a telegraph key, but had, of course, heard the familiar distress signal S.O.S. as it was being pounded out in movies.

To my surprise, Morse code was similar to drumming and learning it wasn't all that difficult. Each letter and number is distinguished by a particular pattern of electrical pulses. This was not going to be that hard, I thought, just practice. And so I did. After a while, I was no longer hearing individual letters, but words.

It wasn't long before I was ready, and I found a local ham who administered that first frightening five-word-per-minute code test and novice written exam, which I passed the first time, thank goodness. After a little more study, I was off to the Federal Communications Commission Office located in Chicago to begin taking additional exams to upgrade my license which would give me more operating privileges on the radio bands.

But my timing was a little off. I got to Chicago at 4:00 AM, nothing was open, and I needed gas and a sandwich. I pulled into a filling station and approached the burglar-proof glass wall counter. The clerk wouldn't even give me change for a $20, so I sat in the car and waited for the sun to come up. I got my gas and sandwich, headed to the FCC in downtown Chicago, took the test, passed it, and headed back home. And that was the beginning of my career in ham radio. I studied and practiced and tested for license upgrades to Advanced Class, then Extra Class.

Whiskey Delta Four Lima Zulu Charlie

After passing the FCC exam that first time, WD4LZC was my official call sign. As I have moved up in licensing over the years by taking and passing more challenging exams, I could have changed my call. However,

I have had it so long that it is almost like my name, so I have simply held on to it over the years. Because L-a-r-n-e-l-l-e is quite long when sending it in code to another operator, I use a shortened form of my middle name: "Stu" (short for Steward) — quick and easy to send and hear.

Radio is more than a hobby for me. It is a social tool. I have friends and make contacts with people all over the world. When I'm sitting at the radio, whether I'm using a microphone or code key, I'm thinking of little else. It's a way to get away, settle down and relax. We are just operators — no Grammy winners or artists, no company presidents or elite athletes — just amateur radio ops getting in shape to handle emergencies, should they arise, by experimentation and having fun.

Changing the World

Amateur radio has been a great addition to my life, and I have learned to communicate in ways that keep me focused and purposeful. I have stayed interested in learning more, constantly improving, and testing. In 2009, I was invited to be part of the 500-member First Class Operators Club that started in the United Kingdom in 1938, and has members all over the world. It was an honor to be sponsored and initiated into this elite club.

I've met hams in Louisville, Kentucky and around the world in places like Sweden and France, Italy and England, Greenland and Brazil, who I probably wouldn't know otherwise because they're not necessarily involved in music. And I happen to think a lot of boundaries get broken down because of these contacts between men and women who have a common interest. The world becomes a very small place on amateur radio. And that's a good thing. Talking about the things we love, bridges gaps between countries and people and ideologies. It is an ever-expanding, no-limits world that still pays attention to the traditional values of courtesy and respect in communicating with people. It is nostalgic, yet advanced; complicated, yet simple. It is fun and challenging, but can quickly become the difference between life and death in the midst of a disaster. I like to believe ham radio can become a microcosm of every personality in the world. Just maybe, we will continue to soften the walls that exist between countries, cultures, races, genders and ages. Somehow, together, I think we can make it work.

Appendix
AWARDS AND HONORS

DOVE AWARDS

1996 Inspirational Album of the Year for Unbelievable Love

1993 Inspirational Album of the Year for Generation 2 Generation

1992 Inspirational Album of the Year for Larnelle Live...Psalms, Hymns & Spiritual Songs

1988 Male Vocalist of the Year

1988 Songwriter of the Year

1988 Inspirational Album of the Year for The Father Hath Provided

1986 Male Vocalist of the Year

1986 Inspirational Album of the Year for I've Just Seen Jesus

1983 Inspirational Black Album of the Year for Touch Me Lord

1983 Male Vocalist of the Year

1981 Contemporary Black Gospel Album of the Year for Give Me More Love in My Heart

GRAMMY AWARDS

1989 Best Gospel Performance, Male for Larnelle…Christmas

1988 Best Gospel Performance, Male for The Father Hath Provided

1986 Best Solo Gospel Performance for "How Excellent Is Thy Name"

1986 Best Gospel Performance by Duo or Group for "I've Just Seen
   Jesus" with Sandi Patty

1984 Best Gospel Performance by Duo or Group for "More Than
   Wonderful" with Sandi Patty

HALL OF FAME INDUCTIONS

2014 Gospel Music Hall of Fame (as a member of Gaither Vocal Band)

2011 Kentucky Music Hall of Fame

2008 Amateur Radio Hall of Fame

2007 Gospel Music Hall of Fame (as solo artist)

#1 HIT RADIO SINGLES

Blessing and Honor

All Along The Way

Walkin' With My Lord

I Don't Know Why You Love Me

Beyond All The Limits

Take The Time

Open Door

I Can Begin Again

Childlike Faith

I Choose Joy

When Praise Demands A Sacrifice

In It After All

I Miss My Time With You

He Loved Me With A Cross

There Stands The Cost

Everything You Are
Didn't You Know
The Father Hath Provided
I've Just Seen Jesus

VARIOUS AWARDS AND HONORS

2016 Heritage Award from the National Convention of Gospel Choirs and Choruses

2014 Kentucky Governor's Award for Lifetime Achievement in the Arts

2008 Honorary Doctorate from Alma Mater, Western Kentucky University

2005 Soul 2 Soul Radio Award

1999 Honorary Doctorate from Campbellsville University

1991 Silver Bell Award for Distinguished Public Service presented by the Ad Council

1989 Cashbox Magazine Award for Contemporary Gospel Single of the Year for "I Can Begin Again"

1988 Stellar Award, Best Solo Performance by Male Contemporary for **The Father Hath Provided** album

1987 Singing News Fan Award for Favorite Black Artist

1986 Singing News Fan Award for Favorite Black Artist

1986 Gospel Music News People's Choice Award for Favorite Black Artist

1985 Singing News Fan Award for Favorite Black Artist

1981 Religion In Media Award

DISCOGRAPHY

2012 **Larnelle Live in Nashville** CD/DVD(Seaboard Records)

2005 **I Want To Be A Star** (produced by Kent Hooper for Discovery House Music)

2002 **The American Spirit** (EP compilation)

2002 **Comfort in the Midst** (compilation)

2002 **Pass the Love** (Produced by David Byerley & Michael Omartian, Crowne Music)

2000 **A Story to Tell-Hymns & Praises** (Produced by Lari Goss, Diadem Records)

1998 **First Love** (Produced by Greg Nelson, Brentwood Records)

1995 **Unbelievable Love** (Produced by Lari Goss, Robert White Johnson, Bill Cuomo)**

1994 **Beyond All The Limits** (Produced by Robert White Johnson, Bill Cuomo, Joe Hogue, Michael Powell)**

1992 **I Choose Joy** (Produced by Joe Hogue and Lari Goss)**

1991 **The Best of 10 Years 1 & 2****

1990 **Larnelle Live…Psalms Hymns & Spiritual Songs** (Produced by Lari Goss)**

1989 **I Can Begin Again** (Produced by Greg Nelson)**

1988 **Larnelle Christmas** (Produced by Greg Nelson)**

1987 **The Father Hath Provided** (Produced by Greg Nelson)**

1986 **From A Servant's Heart** (Produced by Greg Nelson)**

1985 **I've Just Seen Jesus** (Produced by Greg Nelson)**

1982 **Touch Me Lord** (Produced by Greg Nelson)**

1982 **Best Of Larnelle** *

1981 **Give Me More Love In My Heart** (Produced by Howard McCrary and Paul Johnson)*

1978 **Free***

1977 **Larnelle…More** (Produced by Thurlow Spurr and Bob Mackenzie)*

1975 **Tell It To Jesus** (Produced by Bergen White)*

   ** Benson Records

   * Word Records

ABOUT THE AUTHORS

Larnelle Harris

Described by CCM Magazine as having a "larger-than-life stage presence with impeccable vocal prowess," Larnelle Harris has become the epitome of talent and integrity in a career that spans over four decades. He is the only person in history to be a member of the Gospel Music Hall of Fame, the Amateur Radio Hall of Fame and the Kentucky Music Hall of Fame. Larnelle has garnered numerous accolades for his music, including five Grammy Awards, eleven Dove Awards (three of which were for Male Vocalist of the Year), and a Stellar Award, among other honors. He has garnered nineteen #1 radio singles and countless top 10 hits. Songs such as "How Excellent Is Thy Name," "I Miss My Time With You," "I've

Just Seen Jesus," and his signature song, "Amen," are now considered modern classics.

From the White House to the danger zone of the 38th Parallel, Larnelle has impacted audiences across the globe with his music and ministry. He was the first Christian artist to perform inside the Kremlin after the fall of the Soviet Union. He is one of a handful of celebrities to receive the Ad Council's Silver Bell Award for Distinguished Public Service in recognition of his song "Mighty Spirit" as the theme music for the longest-running Public Service Announcement in television history. Larnelle was honored by his home state of Kentucky with the Governor's Lifetime Achievement Award in the Arts, making him the first Christian artist to receive the honor.

Larnelle continues to tour worldwide, with recent dates at Carnegie Hall and in Paris, France. He recently performed for the National Day of Prayer event in Washington D.C. in and sang for a gathering of Ambassadors to the United Nations.

Larnelle and wife, Mitzy, reside in Louisville, Kentucky. Their son, Lonnie, and daughter, Teresa, have families of their own, which means the grandchildren visit often, much to their grandparents delight.

Visit www.Larnelle.com for more information.

Christine Schaub

Christine Schaub is the author of the critically-acclaimed MUSIC OF THE HEART series, including *Finding Anna* — the "rest of the story" behind the writing of the hymn "It Is Well With My Soul," and *The Longing Season* — the story behind "Amazing Grace," with Bethany House Publishers.

Her foray into memoir writing/editing began with singer/speaker Ginger Millermon's 2000 book *Grace Thus Far*, and extended with singer/radio host Shellie Nichol's 2015 book *Destination Hope*.

In 2003, Christine won the "On the Page" screenwriting contest at Screenwriting Expo 2 in Los Angeles. Her one-page story, written on-site in 24 hours for Jacqueline Bisset, was selected by the actress as the best Oscar Wilde-type comedy for her persona.

While working in freelance corporate communications, Christine completed three feature-length screenplays, including a drama/comedy, romantic comedy, and sci-fi action/drama; developed four biopic teleplays for the stories behind the hymns; and published an online column for the MethodX website (Upper Room Ministries).

Christine honed her writing skills after more than 15 years in corporate communications for healthcare, pharmaceutical, and entertainment companies. She has also been a featured conference speaker on working with at-risk youth and changed lives in the classrooms with her creative presentation style. Her love for the arts has taken her from church platforms to civic and professional stages, performing classics and dramas from her own pen.

Christine graduated from Anderson University with a bachelor's degree in Mass Communications. She has served on numerous boards and committees, usually as Communications Chair, and has received both regional and national awards in writing and design.

Morgan James
Speakers Group

www.TheMorganJamesSpeakersGroup.com

We connect Morgan James published authors with live and online events and audiences whom will benefit from their expertise.

Printed in the USA
CPSIA information can be obtained
at www.ICGtesting.com
JSHW021957150824
68134JS00055B/2079

9 781683 505273